Many people today feel that something has gone wrong with British society and British politics. The quality of life seems to be declining. Crime soars. Traffic and pollution spiral. Mass unemployment is undiminished, while many people experience insecurity and stress at work. Growing poverty and inequality have left many of Britain's citizens excluded from mainstream society. Everywhere, the sense of community seems to be breaking down.

In the world as a whole, poverty and conflict cause immense suffering and threaten the security of nations. Global environmental degradation – from the greenhouse effect to the destruction of rainforests – makes the very future of the planet uncertain.

Yet the political system seems barely to register what is happening. It is hardly surprising that public disillusionment with politicians and Parliament has never been higher.

The Politics of the Real World addresses these interlocking crises. Setting out the issues clearly, it explains how conventional economic and social policies are creating the problems we face, not solving them. Arguing that the British political system itself needs rejuvenating, it proposes a new direction for the UK in an increasingly globalised world.

REAL WORLD
is committed to raising the importance of environmental sustainability, social justice – in the UK and internationally – and democratic renewal in UK political debate.

D1355044

The Members of the Real World coalition are:

MICHAEL JACOBS

is an economist and writer whose previous books include
The Green Economy (1991). He is currently Research Fellow in the Department of
Geography, at the London School of Economics and Political Science.

THE POLITICS
OF
THE REAL WORLD

Meeting the New Century

———

Michael Jacobs

———

WRITTEN AND EDITED

FOR THE

Real World

COALITION

EARTHSCAN

Earthscan Publications Ltd, London

First published in the UK 1996 by
Earthscan Publications Limited
Reprinted 1996

A catalogue record for this book is available from the British Library

ISBN: 1 85383 350 9

Typesetting by PCS Mapping & DTP, Newcastle upon Tyne
Page design by S&W Design

Printed in England by Clays Ltd, St Ives plc

Cover design by Andrew Corbett

For a full list of publications please contact:
Earthscan Publications Limited
120 Pentonville Road
London N1 9JN
Tel. (0171) 278 0433
Fax: (0171) 278 1142
Email: sales@earthscan.co.uk

Earthscan Publications Limited is an editorially independent subsidiary of
Kogan Page Limited and publishes in association with the WWF-UK and the
International Institute for Environment and Development.

Contents

Foreword

Real World is a coalition of non-governmental organisations committed to raising the importance of environmental sustainability, social justice – including the relief and eradication of poverty, in this country and internationally – and democratic renewal in UK political debate.

Politics in the UK, not least during elections, has consistently failed to address the critical issues facing the world and facing Britain. Among these are catastrophic global and local environmental degradation; poverty and conflict in the Third World; unemployment, poverty and inequality (including gender and racial inequality) in this country; widespread disaffection with the political system and political parties; a pervasive loss of community. These interconnected crises pose grave threats to human wellbeing and human rights in many parts of the world, to international security for all nations and, in Britain, to the cohesion and stability of society.

Individually, the member organisations of Real World work in one or more of these fields. We have come together out of a recognition that the issues with which we are concerned are related, both nationally and internationally; and that therefore each organisation's particular concerns cannot be addressed adequately unless all of them are.

Real World seeks to get these issues onto the political agenda. But it hopes to do more than this. Its vision is positive: that a political and economic programme based on the goals of sustainability, social justice, democratic renewal and community regeneration can improve the quality of life for people in Britain and can restore a sense of shared purpose and common values to our society. At the same time, such a prgramme can help to improve the lives of people elsewhere in the world, and can begin the urgent task of restoring the integrity and stability of the earth's ecosystems. We believe that this would reduce international conflict and enhance security.

Democratic renewal is not an accidental part of Real World's concerns. We believe that a principal reason that issues of sustainability and social justice are not being addressed is the archaic and constricted framework within which politics in the UK is conducted. Real World seeks the rejuvenation of democratic debate and activity – in Parliament, in local government, in the media and in the wider civil society. In this sense, Real World represents a re-declaration of faith in democracy, in the readiness of people to work together to achieve shared goals, and in the creativity and resilience of the human spirit in meeting today's unprecedented challenges.

Real World's aim is to persuade decision makers and opinion formers, particularly in the media, as to the significance and urgency of the issues we raise, and to generate media coverage for them. We aim to bring pressure to bear on the political parties to bring their policies more into line with the realities of the crises facing us. We hope also to encourage people in general to think afresh about these realities and the values necessary to address them, and to find in these opportunities for new partnerships and new solutions.

We believe that there is a substantial groundswell of public opinion in the UK in favour of a 'new politics' embracing sustainability, social justice, democracy and community regeneration. Real World hopes to provide a strictly non-party political forum in which the new agenda can be articulated, and from which the political system can be influenced. A programme of activities is being organised to promote the goals of Real World and to seek broader support for them.

This book sets out the core thinking that lies behind the Real World initiative. It offers an analysis of the issues with which we are concerned and proposes some directions for reform. Its remit is necessarily wide: it goes well beyond the stated aims and objects of any one of Real World's member organisations. In endorsing this book, each organisation is therefore indicating their formal agreement only in those areas where they have specific competence. At the same time, each endorses the overall argument of the book as a whole. Each also acknowledges the expertise and authority of the other member organisations of Real World in those areas where they themselves do not have specific competence.

John Stewart
Chair,
ALARM UK

Susan Spencer
Chief Executive,
Birmingham Settlement

Judy Ling Wong
Director,
Black Environment Network

John Matthews
Head,
British Association of Settlements
and Social Action Centres

Ian Linden
General Secretary,
Catholic Institute for International
Relations

Andrew Puddephatt
Director,
Charter 88

Michael H Taylor
Director,
Christian Aid

Paul Goggins
National Coordinator,
Church Action on Poverty

John Philpott
Director,
Employment Policy Institute

Sara Parkin and Jonathon Porritt
Directors,
Forum for the Future

Charles Secrett
Executive Director,
Friends of the Earth (England,
Wales and Northern Ireland)

Kevin Dunion
Director,
Friends of the Earth Scotland

Judy Robinson
Director,
Greater Manchester Centre for
Voluntary Organisation

Richard Sandbrook
Executive Director,
International Institute for
Environment and Development

Kenyon E Wright
Director,
KAIROS

Michael Keating
Director,
Media Natura Trust

Martin Hartog
Chair,
Medical Action for Global Security
(MEDACT)

Lib Peck
Director,
National Peace Council

Don Burrows
Chief Executive,
Neighbourhood Initiatives
Foundation

Ed Mayo
Director,
New Economics Foundation

David Bryer
Director,
Oxfam (UK and Ireland)

Peter Beaumont
Director,
Pesticides Trust

Wendy Thomas
Director,
Population Concern

Damian Killeen
Director,
The Poverty Alliance

x

David A. Player

David A Player
Chair,
Public Health Alliance

Mike Aaronson

Mike Aaronson
Director,
Save the Children Fund

T Clunies-Ross

Tracey Clunies-Ross
Chair,
Sustainable Agriculture, Food and
Environment (SAFE) Alliance

C. Tysoe

Colin Tysoe
Chairperson,
Tools for Self Reliance

Stephen Joseph

Stephen Joseph
Director,
Transport 2000

Malcolm Harper

Malcolm Harper
Director,
United Nations Association (UK)

Beth Smith

Beth Smith
General Secretary,
Quaker Social Responsibility and
Education

L Gray

Linda Gray
Director,
Scottish Education and Action for
Development (Sead)

John Grimshaw

John Grimshaw
Director and Chief Engineer,
Sustrans

Tim Cordy

Tim Cordy
Director,
Town and Country Planning
Association

Paul Convery

Paul Convery
Director,
Unemployment Unit

Mike Daligan

Mike Daligan
Director,
Walter Segal Self Build Trust

Dr Simon Lyster
Director General,
Wildlife Trusts

Diana Cripps
Executive Director,
Women's Environmental Network

Barry Coates
Director,
World Development Movement

Robin Pellew
Director,
World Wide Fund for Nature
(WWF) UK

Acknowledgements

Many people have contributed to the production of this book. As it has gone through various drafts it has been assiduously read and commented upon by staff, trustees and management committee members of each of the organisations belonging to Real World. Most of the organisations have contributed a 'Witness Box'. Many other people, from within the organisations and outside, have provided valuable statistical and factual material.

I should like to express my gratitude in particular to the following, whose comments and support throughout the process have been an enormous help: Lindsay Cooke (Charter 88), Peter Madden (Christian Aid), Sara Parkin, Jonathon Porritt (Forum for the Future), Duncan McLaren (FoE), Caroline LeQuesne (Oxfam) and Barry Coates (WWF). The text has also benefited greatly from detailed comments made by Lucy Ackroyd, George Gelber (CAFOD), Ian Linden (CIIR), various staff at Christian Aid, John Philpott, Nick Isles (EPI), Kevin Watkins, Audrey Bronstein (Oxfam), Pat Murray (Population Concern), Damian Killeen (Poverty Alliance), Maggie Winters (PHA), Angela Penrose (SCF), Linda Gray (Sead), Stephen Young (TCPA), Paul Convery (Unemployment Unit), Victor Anderson, Colin Darracott, Paul Ekins, Andrew Glyn, Julian Jacobs and Nick Young.

I am very grateful to all the following for their contributions and assistance: John Stewart (ALARM UK), Judy Ling Wong (BEN), John Matthews (BASSAC), Susan Spencer, Pat Conaty (Birmingham Settlement), Paul Goggins (CAP), Charles Secrett (FoE EWNI), Kevin Dunion (FoE Scotland), Richard Sandbrook, Koy Thomson (IIED), Kenyon Wright (KAIROS), Gillian Reeve (MEDACT), Michael Keating (Media Natura Trust), Helen Foster (NIF), Ed Mayo (NEF), Wendy Thomas (Population Concern), Beth Smith (QSRE),

Vicki Hird, Hugh Raven (SAFE Alliance), Carol Freeman (Sustrans), Tim Cordy (TCPA), Stephen Joseph (Transport 2000), Felix Dodds, Chris Church (UNA).

For providing information, often at short notice, I should like to thank in addition Alex MacGillivray (NEF), Amanda Brace, Andrew Kinnear, Mick O'Connell, Anna Stanford (FoE), Sophia Henderson (Population Concern), Liz Orton, Robert Archer (Christian Aid), Ivan Nutbrown (WDM), Rachel Lampard (CHAS), Lisa Harker (CPAG) and John Hills, along with various extremely helpful but unnamable officials of government departments and international agencies. Andrew Simms and Cleo Cox provided valuable research assistance. Gary Haley drew the graphics and typeset the text. Kate Lamb and Anne Paintin gave superb administrative support. Gary Willis helped to expedite the final stages.

Real World is grateful to Barnardo's, Gallup, the Institute for Public Policy Research, the Joseph Rowntree Foundation, the Joseph Rowntree Reform Trust, MORI, Dartmouth Publishing, the Worldwatch Institute and the World Resources Institute for permission to use published material.

Real World is particularly grateful to Jonathan Sinclair Wilson and Jo O'Driscoll of Earthscan, whose belief, tolerance and energy have brought the book into existence with remarkable speed.

Without the support of Cathy McKenzie it would not have been possible at all.

Michael Jacobs
January 1996

Introduction:
Hope, Fear and the New Century

The year 2000 approaches. The symbolism is irresistible. A new century, a new millennium: a time to take stock of the past, to look forward to the future with hope and purpose.

But nobody could say that this was happening in Britain today. Rather, the country seems to be drifting aimlessly into the 21st century. The body politic frequently seems rudderless, swinging to and fro on passing waves, mesmerised by the smallest movements. The deep ocean currents of global change meanwhile move us powerfully and unnoticed underneath.

There is a significant gap here between politics and people. As 1995's 50th anniversary VE Day commemorations revealed, amongst the public at large there *is* a questioning of where we have come from in this century and where we have reached. Even more, social attitude surveys show, people are looking into the future (see Panel 1). But the clouds on the horizon are dark.

For large numbers in Britain today, the new century is not a source of hope. The predominant mood, if anything, is of fear. People are anxious about the future, about the world they are leaving for their children. They see, with a profound understanding quite missing from national political life, the growing crisis of humankind's impact on the natural environment, as the simultaneous growth of material consumption and population generates inexorably greater pollution and resource degradation. They witness poverty, famine and conflict in distant places and know that we cannot disclaim responsibility. They see the fabric of British society tearing under the strain of inequality and the glorification of me-first materialism. They foresee a world in which people live increasingly barricaded lives, fearful of others, besieged by crime; in which material wealth offers no substitute for the lost quality of community life.

Are we witnessing the first generation in 150 years to believe that 'progress' may have ended; that our children's experience of life will be worse, not better, than our own?

Fear is often accompanied by a feeling of impotence. The forces of change seem so rapid, so uncontrollable. The globalisation of markets and cultures and the increasing international mobility of capital; the shift of economic power from Europe to East Asia; apparently unstoppable technological advance, much of it ethically troubling; the breakdown of traditions and the transformation of social and cultural institutions. All these seem to leave politics flailing.

This would be true even if attention was being paid to the consequences of such change. But it isn't. The real problem is that the British political system seems to express so little understanding or even awareness of what is occurring. Even worse – and this is what stokes the public feeling of impotence – there is no sense of urgency. As an individual country, and as part of humankind as a whole, Britain faces large, difficult problems. The future looks threatening, not hopeful. And yet nowhere in national political life is even a debate occurring. There is little sense of purpose and scant sense of direction. Our politicians and political media sometimes seem not to be living in the real world.

The crisis of British politics has now been well documented.[1] There is widespread and increasing disillusionment, not just with government but with the whole apparatus of politicians and parties, parliament and bureaucracies. This disaffection is partly about form – a reaction to the archaic and alienating nature of the British political system. But it is also about substance. British politics is simply not addressing the large, difficult issues facing us. Indeed, our political structures seem structurally incapable of acting on them. The revitalisation of political debate and political institutions has therefore become an essential element in any wider reassessment of economic and social objectives.

It is for these reasons that many of the UK's non-governmental organisations in the fields of environment, international development, social justice and democratic reform have come together in a new coalition. The name we have chosen reflects our belief that British politics must address

---

Panel 1

Attitudes Towards the Future

In a MORI poll conducted in April 1995, a nationally representative sample of 1069 people aged over 15 was asked: 'Do you think that the kind of world that today's children will inherit will be better or worse than the kind of world that children of your generation inherited, or about the same?' The results were:

Better	12%
Worse	60%
About the same	25%
Don't know	4%

The principal developments or features which people felt were making the world worse were the level of crime, availability of illegal drugs, the breakdown in family structures, unemployment rates, the risk of contracting HIV/AIDS and pollution and environmental degradation.

A similar poll was conducted by Gallup in March–April 1995. Their sample (1050 people aged over 16) was asked: 'Do you think that children today have a better future in front of them than you had when you were a child, a worse future, or about the same?' The overall results were:

Better	18%
Worse	63%
About the same	15%
Don't know	4%

The large majority for 'Worse' occurred in all age groups except for those aged 65 and over, and all social classes and regions. Parents of children under 16 were particularly pessimistic.

Sources: MORI poll conducted for Barnardo's and published in *The Facts of Life: The Changing Face of Childhood* (London: Barnardo's, 1995). Gallup poll conducted for and published in M Young and A H Halsey, *Family and Community Socialism* (London: Institute for Public Policy Research, 1995). Qualitative research into attitudes and values reveals similar pessimism about the future, again related to crime, job insecurity and environmental degradation. See for example P Macnaghten *et al*, *Sustainability and Public Perceptions in Lancashire* (Preston: Lancashire County Council, 1995).

---

itself to the problems of the real world which face us. We believe that this requires a new understanding of the nature of economic and social progress, and the mechanisms of political change. We believe, moreover, that this can only be done if the processes and institutions of democracy in Britain are rejuvenated.

The Real World coalition represents a new departure for most of our member organisations. In the past we have largely been separate, working on more or less tightly defined groups of issues. But it has become increasingly clear that these issues are linked: caused by the same processes and governed by the same policy assumptions. Addressing one set of interests is therefore no longer enough. Each organisation's particular concerns will not be tackled adequately unless all of them are. We have recognised that we must show how these concerns are connected; and therefore how they require a wider and deeper approach to solving them.

In bringing together organisations concerned with poverty in the Third World and poverty in Britain, for example, it has become evident how similar are the causes of the issues with which they deal. In both cases poverty results from the marginalisation of particular regions and neighbourhoods by the forces of global competition; in both cases it is the efforts of communities themselves which are the principal focus of change. In both cases – contrary to widespread belief – environmental improvement and poverty eradication go together, since the poor almost always live in the worst environments. This has generated new connections between environmental organisations and those concerned principally with social justice: the two aims go hand in hand. And increasingly throughout this process it has become clear how the particular structures and practices of politics in Britain militate against change, whether at an international or community level; and therefore the role that democratic renewal must play in achieving the substantive ends of sustainability and social justice.

Real World has come into being to get these issues and this understanding onto the political agenda, and thereby to influence change. This document is an attempt to set out our position. Its analysis comes from the experience of the organisations which make up the coalition, and that of the people with and through whom we work. It is these experiences, we believe, which give us our authority to speak. The members and supporters of Real World's constituent organisations together number approximately 2.1 million.[2] These are ordinary people who wish to see change, and who are prepared to support their beliefs financially and through various kinds of non-party political activity. Many of Real World's organisations moreover work more widely with other community groups, both in this country and elsewhere in the world. These groups too are made up of ordinary people, trying to improve their own conditions of life and those of others. Their voices are not often heard amidst the noise of Westminster politics.

If it is these voices which give us authority, they also give us hope. For it is in the activities of non-governmental and community organisations, in Britain and around the globe, that positive change is most evident. Often against powerful odds, and with few resources, such groups are finding creative and lasting ways of making their – and therefore our – world better. We seek to give this hope a wider articulation in British politics.

This book is primarily an analysis, not a set of solutions. The first step to a politics of the real world, we believe, is an understanding of what the problems are, and why they are occurring. Nevertheless we do offer in each section the broad approach we believe is required to address the problems. We do not pretend to have all the solutions; and we recognise that profound questions remain. But we believe that these must be debated, not ignored.

To such a debate we offer, finally, a vision. We believe that the coming of a new century should be perceived as a time of hope and of purpose. Fear and despair can only be self-fulfilling. We have a profound belief in the capacity of the human spirit to meet the challenges facing us. Our children are not condemned to live in a frightening and hopeless future. It can be changed.

Succeeding to Fail:
Questioning Progress

The Dominant Model

Since the end of the Second World War the industrialised world has had few doubts about the nature of economic and social progress – or indeed, about our achievement of it. Unprecedented material affluence, significant advances in health care, the widespread extension of tertiary education, extraordinary technological innovation, the consolidation of liberty and democracy, the flourishing of popular culture: with such success, few have questioned either goal or method. Indeed, the model of progress has been adopted not just in the originally industrialised North, but by almost every country in the world. The fall of the Berlin Wall seemed merely to confirm the triumph of the Western idea. With the exception of some Islamic states, and with minor variations between countries, almost the entire planet is now bound up in a single, global process of economic and social development. To many it seems that the great struggles over political purpose are now finished.[1]

The economic and political structures of global and national 'development' are very powerful: their dynamism and resilience help to explain their success. But perhaps even more powerful is the conceptual framework underlying and informing the structures. The dominant intellectual model of economic and social progress has had an extraordinary grip not just on politicians, economists and policy makers but, in turn, on the mental pictures of the general public. It has governed our understanding both of the objectives of 'development' and of the mechanisms required to achieve it.

Broadly speaking, the model can be described as follows. The principal purpose of economic activity is to raise incomes. Income growth makes people better off: it enables them to consume greater quantities of both material and non-material goods, and through taxation enables governments to provide essential public services such as education, health care and social security. For individuals access to income is gained through waged employment. Given technological improvements to productivity, annual economic growth not only generates jobs, but is required to sustain them.

The motor of growth is free trade: as import duties, foreign exchange controls and other forms of protection are lowered, goods, capital and labour flow to where they are most productive, and more wealth is generated. Poverty is gradually reduced, as incomes circulate from richer areas to poorer ones. In the South (the Third World), as in the industrialised North before it, free trade and growth lead to 'modernisation' – the increasing productivity of agriculture, the movement of people into towns and cities and the transformation from traditional to modern cultures. In the North, and in the South to come, scientific advance drives technological change, and thence both economic growth and social development. Social and environmental problems, for example, are gradually tackled, as resources are generated to deal with them and market and institutional failures rectified.

This model of development has never of course been wholly consensual. Important differences have separated Left and Right: notably on the relative sizes of the private and public sectors, and on the degree of regulation and planning of markets. The Left has generally argued for proactive governmental measures to redistribute wealth, at least domestically; the Right for the priority of wealth generation through free markets – although, significantly, the original East Asian 'tiger' economies have combined conservative ideology with highly interventionist economic strategies. But these differences have rested on an underlying model of economic growth and social progress which has not by and large been in dispute.

In the 1980s a particular form of the model became dominant in most Northern countries, and in the international institutions governed by them. The objective of full employment, a keystone of policy in industrialised countries after the War, was abandoned. The control of inflation replaced the stimulation of demand as the principal policy instrument to generate growth. Markets have been deregulated, and publicly owned enterprises and services privatised. Increasing reliance has been placed on private provision of welfare services, for example in education, health care and pensions, as public spending has been reduced. Economic and social policies based on these principles have been applied not just in the North – the UK being a prominent example – but in the South, as the condition of development aid and finance provided by the International Monetary Fund, the World Bank and bilateral financial institutions.

In some countries, for some people, implementation of the development model – particularly in its pre-1980s form – has been unquestionably successful. Over the past two decades, consistently high growth rates in East Asia (where markets have in general not been deregulated or public spending reduced) have turned recently 'underdeveloped' countries into economic powerhouses now exceeding some of their Northern competitors in average per capita incomes and in industrial strength. In many countries of the South, economic growth has helped to improve educational levels, health care and social provision. In the North, until recently, poverty and deprivation showed a steady decline; cultural liberation, particularly that of women, appeared to accompany continuing material affluence.

Questioning the Model

But the model has been developing cracks. For a start, large numbers of people have not benefited from its implementation. The number of people in the world living in absolute poverty has grown, not declined, in the last 25 years.[2] While East Asia has experienced rapid economic growth, the last decade has seen a decline in output and incomes throughout sub-Saharan Africa. In much of Latin America, economic growth at the national level has been accompanied by vastly increased levels of poverty. At a lower but no less significant rate the same pattern of increasingly unequal growth has been true of Britain, the United States and many other Northern countries. The theory that wealth would automatically 'trickle down' from rich to poor has been proved simply wrong: rather, it now appears that wealth can circulate and expand within geographical and economic class boundaries to the exclusion of those outside.

In fact a more profound questioning is now evident. It is a commonplace of recent economic and political commentary in Britain that substantial economic growth has not generated the expected 'feelgood factor'. Even amongst those benefiting from greater material affluence, it seems, there is dissatisfaction. People appear to be concerned, not just about having more money, but about aspects of wellbeing for which private income is little help: the increased insecurity of employment, for example; the rise in crime, the effects of air pollution on children's health. Moreover there seems to be an insistent anxiety about a decline in what is called the 'social fabric': a sense that growing inequality and the perceived loss of 'community' are damaging the character of British society as a whole. Measures of social wellbeing which go beyond income alone appear to confirm this feeling that the quality of life is getting worse rather than better.[3]

Meanwhile, environmental problems have not been solved in the way the model predicts. Over the last 20 years new and larger problems have appeared. Many of them seem resistant to the traditional method of add-on technological solutions. The greenhouse effect, depletion of the ozone layer and the loss of biodiversity threaten the fundamental life support systems of the planet. Inexorable traffic growth, with its associated costs in congestion, air pollution and the loss of countryside from road building, challenges one of the cherished achievements of modern society, mass car ownership. The institutions of political regulation seem barely capable of handling such central, global and long-term issues.

Once upon a time, Third World poverty, relative deprivation in Britain and environmental damage were sources of concern to the mainstream of politics, but not fundamental anxiety. They could be represented either as legacies of pre-industrial society which further economic development would gradually eradicate, or as small and reparable faults in the model which would be solved once economic growth and technological advance had generated the necessary resources and knowledge. But such arguments are no longer tenable. For in too many areas the problems have been getting worse, not better. There is now little sign – indeed, increasingly, little pretence – that such problems will be either eradicated or repaired simply by further application of the model's prescriptions.

On the contrary: what has now become clear is that further economic development on the pattern of the past will continue to exacerbate these problems. For they are not, as supposed, symptoms of the model's *failure*, but of its *success*. The conventional wisdom needs to be exactly reversed: the better the model performs, the *worse* these problems will get. They are endemic, not incidental. Moreover, since each is related to the others, they cannot simply be dealt with separately and incrementally. They require more fundamental changes in the patterns of economic and social development, and therefore in our understanding of what constitutes progress. In the absence of such change, these problems threaten to undermine the genuine successes which have been achieved.

A Different Perspective

From this foundation, the argument of this document is two-fold. First, the costs of the dominant model are ethically unacceptable. It might once have been argued that the costs of poverty and environmental degradation were temporary and outweighed by the benefits they generated. Yes, some people and the natural world lost out in the creation of material affluence, but this would not last long, and it was a price worth paying. But this argument was never morally tolerable, and it is now indefensible. When 35,000 of the world's children die *each day* from preventable hunger and disease;[4] when increasing inequality in Britain is leaving large numbers of the poor and unemployed permanently excluded from mainstream society; when human degradation of the environment is destroying the livelihoods and health of hundreds of millions of people in rich and poor countries, urban and rural areas alike – and when all these costs are getting larger, not smaller; then the morality of the cost-benefit calculus has reached its limit. The beneficiaries of global development patterns are too few, and so many of their material gains too unnecessary, to impose such terrible costs on others. Allowing the rich to get even richer, while the poor grow more numerous and their most basic needs go unmet, is morally barbarous, and it should no longer be accepted.

If this argument is not sufficient, there is a second which appeals to self-interest. For the costs of the dominant model of global economic development are now beginning to outweigh its benefits, even for its beneficiaries. Both in Britain and in the world as a whole poverty is economically inefficient, wasting resources and generating unproductive social costs. Throughout Europe environmental degradation now damages the quality of life even of the affluent, as air pollution, traffic congestion, loss of countryside, chemicalised food production methods and other costs increasingly impinge on everyday life. Crime and social disintegration, once held at bay on the margins of society, have gradually come to corrode the daily experience of millions of ordinary average-income families.

Meanwhile, on a global scale, the combination of poverty, population growth and environmental degradation increasingly threatens the security of nations. Conflicts over resources, and the political instability which arises from population migration, are at present mainly regional phenomena. But as their root causes become more critical, they will not continue to be so confined. The implications for security, immigration and aid spending in the industrialised world are just beginning to be recognised.

The argument, therefore, is not simply that the dominant patterns of economic development, in Britain and in the world as a whole, are wrong morally. It is that they are now counter-productive. They are no longer generating net benefits, but net costs; and these costs are increasing. Change is therefore imperative. This change needs to be not just in the patterns of economic development, but in the model which informs them. We need to reassess what we mean by economic and social progress; and to move to a path more likely to achieve it.

The Environmental Imperative:
Towards Sustainability

The New Challenge

In 1988 Margaret Thatcher made a now-famous speech in which she acknowledged that global climate change presented a new and very serious challenge for humankind. In words which echoed those of the environmental movement itself ('We do not have a freehold on the earth,' she said, 'only a full repairing lease') the then Prime Minister declared that we were experimenting with the very life support systems of the planet.[1]

In the years since then it has become increasingly impossible to argue that the environment is of marginal public or political concern. 'Environmental issues' keep hitting the front pages: one month the depletion of fish stocks and resultant conflicts over fishing rights in European (and Canadian) waters; the next, ozone smog, traffic congestion and the asthma epidemic. Protests over veal crates give way to anxieties about reduced sperm counts, the health effects of pesticides, skin cancers from the depletion of the ozone layer, local fears about waste incineration. Recent years have seen a succession of 'hottest months on record', in 1995 accompanied by one of the worst summer droughts (extending in Yorkshire well into the winter, not to say into public acrimony). Public protests over road-building – Twyford Down, Wanstead, Glasgow, Blackburn, Newbury – have become virtually a constant.

Environmental issues have seeped onto the business pages too. Corporate exposure to environmental liabilities has begun to affect balance sheets and share prices, while significantly increased insurance premiums are now revealed as the first major consequence of global warming.[2] The Brent Spar controversy in 1995 demonstrated the issues vividly. The scientific arguments may have been disputed; but for the public the disposal of a particular oil platform symbolised the wider relationship between industrial society and the natural world. As industry has been forced to recognise, public concern about the environment must now be regarded as a major factor in business – and political – planning.

Understanding of environmental problems has changed (see Panels 2 and 3). It used to be thought that the depletion of finite fossil fuels and minerals was the principal issue. What we now know is that the loss of renewable resources – trees, soils, water, fish – is far more urgent. Renewables do not have to be depleted: if harvest rates equal regeneration rates, a constant stock of the resource can be maintained. But too often consumption vastly outweighs regeneration, leaving degraded land and future scarcity. Pollution too has assumed a greater importance. The problem of fossil fuels is not so much their running out as the damage they cause: the greenhouse effect resulting from carbon emissions, acid rain from sulphur and nitrogen. Local air pollutants, such as lead and hydrocarbons from traffic, are major sources of respiratory disease. More widely, the accumulation in the environment of pesticides, dioxins, PCBs and other toxic chemicals generates health hazards still not fully understood, but of increasing concern.[3] Meanwhile the decline in biodiversity – in the number and variety of the earth's animal and plant species – represents a multiple loss: to the reservoir of genetic material from which new drugs and other products are derived; to the enrichment which nature brings to the wealth of every culture, and to so many people's personal experience; and to the value of the natural world simply of itself.

As regular reports from official agencies show, many of the most serious environmental problems, both globally and in the UK, are getting worse, not better.[4] In many cases (such as with CFCs and the ozone layer) it is the cumulative impact which matters, so even a reduction in the annual rate of damage is not of itself sufficient to alleviate concern. Indeed, the increasing seriousness of environmental trends suggests that what at first looks like a multiplicity of separate problems should in fact be seen as merely different facets of a single, more general one.

What is gradually becoming clear is that current patterns of resource use and waste generation in industrialised societies are not *sustainable*. They give rise to forms of environmental degradation which on current

Panel 2

The Global Environment

The scientific consensus on global climate change is represented by the findings of the Intergovernmental Panel on Climate Change (IPCC), comprising several hundred of the world's leading atmospheric scientists. The IPCC has confirmed the very strong likelihood that global warming will occur as a result of emissions of 'greenhouse gases' – particularly carbon dioxide (CO_2), methane and CFCs. The IPCC estimates that if current emissions trends continue, global mean temperatures are likely to rise at a rate of around 0.3°C per decade – a global warming rate faster than at any time over the past 10,000 years. At this rate, mean temperatures would rise by about 1°C by 2025 and 3°C before the end of the next century. Sea levels would rise approximately 65cm by 2100. There has already been a noticeable rise in global temperatures over recent decades, as increasing emissions of CO_2 have raised atmospheric concentrations.

The release of chlorofluorocarbons (CFCs) into the upper atmosphere continues to cause depletion of the ozone layer, with a 'hole' appearing in 1995 over the Arctic as well as the Antarctic. The increased ultra-violet radiation occuring as a result of ozone depletion raises the incidence of skin cancers and cataracts and has a number of ecological effects. However, as a result of the 1987 international Montreal Protocol, the production of new CFCs is being phased out. If countries comply with their treaty obligations, it is estimated that ozone levels will begin to rise again after about 1998, though chlorine concentrations will not return to their 1970s level (before the first ozone hole appeared) until about 2050.

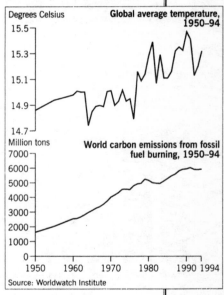

Source: Worldwatch Institute

During the 1980s, the world lost about 8% of its tropical forests – an area almost three times the size of France. The principal causes, varying in different countries, are commercial logging, ranching and population resettlement. As well as being home to many indigenous peoples, tropical forests absorb CO_2, thus reducing global warming, and are the potentially sustainable source of many drugs and industrial products such as rubber, oils and resins. Rainforest destruction is responsible for much of the loss of the world's 'biodiversity', the variety of species it contains. Species loss is now occuring much faster than its 'natural' evolutionary rate, principally as a result of habitat destruction and the introduction of new species by human activity. Projections based on current trends suggest that between 1 and 11% of the world's species per

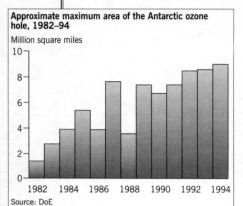

Approximate maximum area of the Antarctic ozone hole, 1982–94

Million square miles

Source: DoE

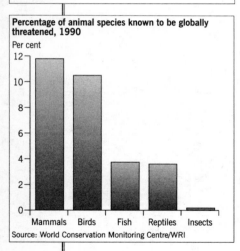

Percentage of animal species known to be globally threatened, 1990

Per cent

Source: World Conservation Monitoring Centre/WRI

decade will be committed to extinction between 1975 and 2015. Globally, about 12% of mammal species and 11% of bird species are categorised as 'threatened'.

The Food and Agriculture Organisation of the UN reports that in four of the world's seventeen major marine fishing areas catches now exceed the 'maximum sustainable yield', leading to stock depletion. Fish catches are declining in a further six areas. Most traditional fish stocks have reached 'full exploitation', meaning that an intensified fishing effort will not increase the catch, and new fishing methods aimed at doing so will cause a reduction in the stock.

Water scarcity is becoming an increasing problem in particular parts of the world. 26 countries, home to 230 million people, are categorised as 'water-scarce', having less than 1,000 cubic metres of annual supplies available per person. By 2000, a third of the population of Africa will live in water-scarce countries. Declining water tables, indicating unsustainable water use, are now evident in parts of China, India, Mexico, the Western US, North Africa and the Middle East. In addition the UN Environment Programme categorises 70% of the world's drylands as suffering from desertification, with about 1.5 million hectares of irrigated lands lost annually to salinisation. In most countries of Africa, where land degradation is particularly widespread, per capita food production has been stagnant or declining over the past decade.

Acidification, caused by pollution from sulphur and nitrogen oxide emissions, ozone and heavy metals, is now affecting forests throughout the world. 22% of European forests are damaged, with most countries experiencing deterioration in the last decade. Acid rain affects 14% of the land area of China. With sulphur-rich coal combustion projected to increase there by 35% during this decade, this will almost certainly rise. Air and water pollution and the production of hazardous wastes are increasing rapidly in almost all industrialising countries. A particular concern is the increasing use of pesticides. While chemical fertilisers, irrigation and high yield crop varieties have enabled agricultural productivity to increase, they have also made crops more vulnerable to pest attack. The consequent rise in pesticide use has led to extremely serious ecological and health problems. Yet pests can quickly become resistant, setting up a 'treadmill' of increasing use. In the 50 years since pesticide use became widespread, the percentage of crop loss from pest damage has not measurably declined.

Sources: IPCC, *Climate Change: The IPCC Scientific Assessment* (Cambridge: Cambridge University Press, 1990); World Resources Institute, *World Resources 1992–93* (Oxford: Oxford University Press, 1992); World Resources Institute, *World Resources 1994–95* (Oxford: Oxford University Press, 1994); L Brown *et al* (eds)/Worldwatch Institute, *Vital Signs 1993–94* (London: Earthscan, 1993); L Brown *et al* (eds)/Worldwatch Institute, *Vital Signs 1995–96* (London: Earthscan, 1995); M Tolba *et al* (eds), *The World Environment 1972–92* (London: Chapman & Hall/UN Environment Programme, 1992); Department of the Environment, *Digest of Environmental Statistics No 17 1995* (London: HMSO, 1995).

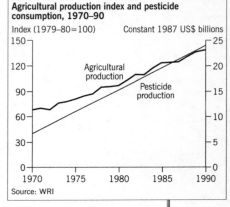

Agricultural production index and pesticide consumption, 1970–90

Source: WRI

trends will have serious and possibly catastrophic consequences for humanity; in some cases, for the whole of the living world. At a minimum, continued pollution and resource depletion will cause widespread damage to human health and to the quality of life. Indeed, this is already happening, to different degrees in different parts of the world – including the UK. At worst, the projections are for global climate change, population movements, loss of agricultural production and breakdown in food chains on a disastrous scale, potentially within the next 20 or 30 years.[5]

The concept of 'sustainability' is at root a simple one. It rests on the acknowledgement, long familiar in economic life, that maintaining income over time requires that the capital stock is not run down. The natural environment performs the function of a capital stock for the human economy, providing essential resources and services, including the assimilation of wastes. Economic activity is presently running down this stock. While in the short term this can generate economic wealth, in the longer term (like selling off the family silver) it reduces the capacity of the environment to provide these resources and services at all. Sustainability is thus the goal of 'living within our environmental means'. Put another way, it implies that we should not pass the costs of present activities onto future generations.

The UK Environment

Most of the most serious environmental problems in the UK continue to get worse. Stronger regulatory regimes in the last decade have led to some important improvements: for example, in overall river water quality (though some rivers are becoming more polluted) and in the emissions of certain pollutants, such as sulphur dioxide, which causes acid rain. But in most other fields the trends remain downward.

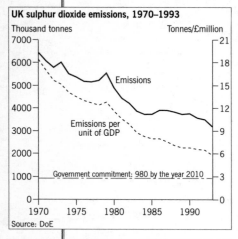

UK sulphur dioxide emissions, 1970–1993

Thousand tonnes — Tonnes/£million

Emissions

Emissions per unit of GDP

Government commitment: 980 by the year 2010

Source: DoE

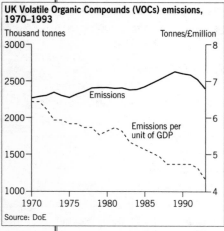

UK Volatile Organic Compounds (VOCs) emissions, 1970–1993

Thousand tonnes — Tonnes/£million

Emissions

Emissions per unit of GDP

Source: DoE

Urban air pollution is a source of particular concern because of its health effects. Overall trends are impossible to estimate with certainty because of shortage of data. But in most of the last few years most UK cities have at some time experienced levels of nitrogen oxides (NO_x) exceeding the Department of Environment's 'poor' air quality threshold (100 ppb). Similarly, ground-level ozone concentrations have exceeded the EC Directive Health Protection Threshold (8 hour mean 50 ppb) on multiple occasions at most urban monitoring sites. Levels of particulates and various 'volatile organic compounds' or VOCs (such as benzene) are also of concern. Alongside industrial emissions, the main cause of these pollutants is road traffic. Emissions from traffic have been rising steadily over the last thirty years in line with road use. Improvements in engine technologies (such as catalytic converters) have cut emissions per kilometre travelled, but by nothing like as much as the total number of kilometres has increased. So total emissions continue to rise.

These graphs illustrate an important lesson. Environmental regulations tend to focus on improving technologies. Such technologies reduce emission levels per unit of output. But this will not cause total pollution to fall if output rises more quickly. In the case of sulphur dioxide, the improvement in 'environmental efficiency' (emissions per unit of output) has been sufficient to cause a decline in total emissions. But in the case of

VOCs, it hasn't: emissions per unit of output are falling, but output is rising faster. So the absolute level of emissions continues to increase. It is the absolute level, of course, which is what counts as far as health and environmental quality are concerned. In transport (road kilometres travelled), there has been no noticeable increase in environmental efficiency at all: as GDP rises, so does traffic. The same relationship applies to solid waste: the more the economy grows, the more waste we produce. The level of waste recycling is much too low to compensate. In the case of aluminium, the amount of recycled material used is rising. But total consumption is rising faster. So as a percentage, recycling is falling: that is, primary or virgin consumption of aluminium continues to increase. In fact for most metals, even the absolute amounts of scrap used are falling. Only for paper and board is the percentage of recycled materials rising (by 4% between 1984 and 1993), thereby allowing a reduction in virgin paper consumption.

The UK's contribution to global warming comes mainly from its carbon dioxide emissions. These fell during the first half of the 1980s, reflecting an improvement in the overall energy efficiency of the UK economy. But this improvement petered out in the 1990s and emissions levelled off. After falling during the recession of 1991–94, CO_2 emissions are now projected to rise again. The Government has offered a number of projections for future emissions. The 'High' scenario given in the figure assumes that economic growth will proceed at 2.85%pa up to 2020, and fuel prices will be relatively high. The 'Low' scenario assumes growth of 1.75%, with relatively low fuel prices.

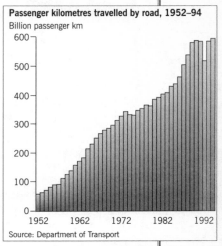

Passenger kilometres travelled by road, 1952–94
Billion passenger km

Source: Department of Transport

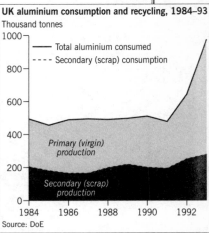

UK aluminium consumption and recycling, 1984–93
Thousand tonnes

— Total aluminium consumed
- - - Secondary (scrap) consumption

Primary (virgin) production

Secondary (scrap) production

Source: DoE

The Government is committed to a target of restoring CO_2 emissions to 1990 levels by 2005. This is achieved in the 'Low' scenario, but not in the 'High'. In both, however, emissions rise after 2005. To make a serious contribution to reducing global warming, Friends of the Earth have proposed a more stringent target of reducing CO_2 emissions by 30% (from 1990 levels) by 2005, followed by further cuts towards the IPCC 60% reduction level.

The loss of natural habitats and species shows little sign of abating. As Britain's land area has become gradually more urbanised (in England, at a rate of 11,000 hectares per annum:

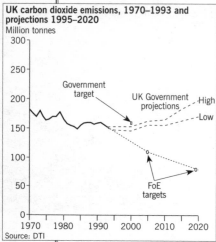

UK carbon dioxide emissions, 1970–1993 and projections 1995–2020

Million tonnes

Source: DTI

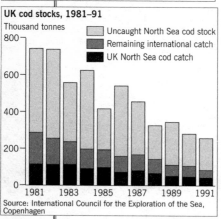

UK cod stocks, 1981–91

Thousand tonnes

- Uncaught North Sea cod stock
- Remaining international catch
- UK North Sea cod catch

Source: International Council for the Exploration of the Sea, Copenhagen

a total of 705,000 hectares of rural land has been lost since 1945), and as agricultural methods have become more intensive, many of Britain's animal and plant species have suffered decline. The Royal Society for the Protection of Birds estimates that 19 bird species (out of a total of about 210) have declined in numbers by 50% or more in the last 25 years, while 18 butterfly species (out of 59) have undergone similarly substantial losses. Giving a rare natural habitat the designation of 'Site of Special Scientific Interest' (SSSI) does not protect it: in 1992–93 over 23,000 hectares of SSSIs were damaged by development, pollution and agricultural activities, and many more are threatened.

The UK's renewable resources are also being depleted. Water consumption has been rising at a time of declining rainfall, leaving several regions of the country needing imports of water to meed demand. North Sea fish stocks are on a long-term downward trend, despite increasingly stringent fishing quotas.

Sources: Department of the Environment, *Digest of Environmental Statistics No 16* 1994 and *No 17* 1995 (London: HMSO, 1994, 1995); National Environmental Technology Centre, *Air Pollution in the UK: 1993/94* (Culham: AEA Technology, 1995); DTI, *Energy Projections for the UK, Energy Paper 65* (London: HMSO, 1995); Environmental Challenge Group, *Environmental Measures* (London: FoE, IIED, NEF, RSBC, RSPB, WWF, WCL, 1994) (all data except RSPB estimates collated from government and statutory agency sources); G Sinclair, *The Lost Land* (London: Council for the Protection of Rural England, 1992).

By the same token, *un*sustainability implies that there are limits to acceptable environmental impacts. That is, there are maximum safe or permissible rates of carbon dioxide emission, deforestation, solid waste generation, water extraction and so on, beyond which it would be intolerably damaging or hazardous to go. The idea of environmental limits has historically been an uncomfortable one, largely through its association with the 'limits to growth' thesis. But this confuses two sorts of growth. How far environmental improvement can be compatible with economic growth is a complex question we shall discuss in a moment. The argument here is simpler.

It is merely that humankind cannot go on polluting and degrading the natural environment at the current rate: at some point the damage caused will certainly overwhelm any possible human benefits and may impair the basic life support systems of the planet. These environmental limits must be scientifically informed, dependent on knowledge of biophysical processes which we do not control and can only partially influence. But they must be politically chosen, the result of social decisions about tolerable and intolerable effects. In this sense, there can be little doubt that society must live within environmental limits: this is a consequence of accepting that current trends of degradation cannot continue. The central questions are, in fact, more difficult: how we determine where those limits lie, and what 'living within them' in practice involves.

The Implications of Environmental Limits

Three kinds of answer have become clear in recent years. The first of these is that reducing the environmental impacts of industrial societies will require fundamental change in economic structures and processes. This is true for a simple (but inescapable) physical reason: there can be no economic activity without the consumption of environmental resources and the discharge of wastes. Despite the habit of conventional economic analysis to ignore this, it is economic activity which causes environmental damage.

But even more importantly, such damage is closely tied to the particular forms and structures of modern economic life. Most of the most serious environmental problems we face are not the result of technical failures in basically sound activities, but flow from the essential character of current production and consumption patterns. It is for this reason that they offer such a challenge to the dominant model.

Global warming, for example, derives from the engine of modern economies, the consumption of fossil fuels. Further economic growth on the current path – in both already-industrialised countries such as the UK, and in the newly industrialising countries such as China, India, Indonesia and Brazil – can only lead to higher carbon dioxide emissions. It *is* possible to decouple emissions from economic growth in the short and medium term, but this will involve quantum changes in the efficiency of production and consumption and in the technologies of energy generation.

Similarly, the exponential increase in traffic on Britain's roads is tightly bound to prevailing patterns of economic development, involving the dispersal of populations out of city centres, increasing journey times to work, shopping and leisure activities, and longer distances travelled by retail goods. The problems of intensive and chemicalised agriculture – pesticide pollution, nitrates in groundwater, animal diseases and cruelty – are not incidental by-products of modern food production but inevitable consequences of it. The loss of biodiversity throughout the world, including Britain, inevitably follows the appropriation of land for industrial and urban development and for large-scale agriculture. Current patterns of international trade help to stimulate each of these problems, and others.

The centrality of environmental damage to prevailing forms of economic development means that these problems cannot be solved – as the dominant model supposes – simply by additional doses of regulation and the application of 'end-of-pipe', clean-up technologies. Nor is it any use waiting for growth to release resources to deal with them. Such growth – in current patterns – will exacerbate rather than alleviate the problems. Those patterns must be changed, not accelerated.

This in turn requires that environmental concerns are placed at the heart of economic policy. The conventional separation of these two fields can no longer be sustained. Only if economic analyses, objectives and strategies incorporate environmental ones can the necessary shifts in the patterns of economic development be understood, and then be brought about.

A second answer to the question of environmental limits follows from this. Such limits make new demands on politics. They force us, to start with, to address our relationship to future generations. Previously this issue could be ducked: the dominant model assumed that economic growth would automatically make the future richer than the past, so the wellbeing of the next generation needed no attention beyond what would provide for the present. But the unsustainability of continuing environmental degradation throws this assumption into reverse. Accepting environmental limits raises explicitly the question of how our current actions will affect the lives of our children and grandchildren, and theirs.

The problem, however, is that in many cases it is not known precisely what these effects will be. The most serious environmental issues are characterised by both complexity and uncertainty. We do not know enough about the way the biosphere works, or the consequences of our interactions with it. Yet it is clear that some of the worst-case risks we face – from the greenhouse effect, for example; from genetic engineering, from the use of chemicals in agriculture and from toxic wastes – are very large.

These circumstances have significant implications for the processes of policy making. They reinforce the importance of applying the 'precautionary principle': erring on the side of environmental safety when risks are large and knowledge uncertain. In some cases this means raising safety standards; in others, simply delaying permission for new technological processes until the consequences are better understood. They warn too against an overconfident reliance on technological fixes, universally applied. Diverse and decentralised policy measures tend to be more robust and less vulnerable to catastrophic mistakes. Changing basic processes to avoid damage occurring (such as in agriculture and industrial pollution) is almost always safer than designing ever more complex means of controlling it.

Perhaps most importantly, the complexity and uncertainty of environmental issues make it imperative that the processes of governance are open and plural. Political centralisation, official secrecy and bureaucratic rigidity are the enemies of effective policy making. They magnify risks, reduce the range of options considered and tested, and increase public alienation from (and therefore resistance to) the political process. In this as in other fields, basic democratic reforms – freedom of information, participatory political and administrative structures, the right to legal redress for harms done – therefore become essential requirements for decision-making. Decisions on where acceptable environmental limits lie – decisions which will affect future generations as much as ourselves – can only be made through open, informed public debate. The environmental crisis in this sense represents not just a challenge for policy, but for the institutions and processes of government itself.

The third element which must be addressed in any answer to the question of environmental limits concerns the relationship of the environment to poverty. It used to be thought that environmental protection was against the interests of the poor. What the poor needed – in the Third World, and in Britain – was economic and employment growth, and these could only be retarded by excessive concern for trees, animals, water quality and so on. We now know however that almost exactly the reverse is the case. The poorest people almost always live in the worst environments. In the rural areas of the developing world they have been forced onto marginal lands by the processes of enclosure, leading to deforestation, soil erosion, agricultural failure and increasing poverty. In urban areas they die from the diseases of water pollution and insanitary waste disposal, and from the air pollution emitted by unregulated factories. Global warming will affect the world's poor – those least able to protect themselves against crop failures and rising sea levels – far more severely than the more affluent.[6]

Similarly, in the United Kingdom the greatest beneficiaries of energy efficiency measures would be the 'fuel poor', the six million people who live in uninsulated homes with inadequate heating systems, who cannot afford to be warm.[7] Air pollution has contributed to a nationwide epidemic of respiratory disease – but this affects poorer families much more than affluent ones.[8] And it is the poorest households, those without access to a car, which have suffered most from the decline in public transport and the dispersal of shopping and leisure facilities.

For this reason, environmentalism is not just a 'middle class' movement, in either North or South. Living within environmental limits involves crucial questions of distribution between nations and social groups; but it does not make environmentalism the enemy of the poor. To be sure, particular policy measures can have adverse distributional effects; but that is a reason to integrate anti-poverty concerns into environmental policy, not to abandon either. Indeed, as public outrage over the imposition of VAT on domestic fuel showed convincingly, environmental protection will not win public support if it does not embody social protection too.

From Population to Consumption

These features of the environmental imperative – the concept of 'sus-

Environment and Community
By the World Wide Fund for Nature UK

The challenge of caring for the environment demands a new ethic for living sustainably, from the local to the global level. There is cause for optimism. In diverse communities across the world, people are creating real and practical solutions to the dilemmas of development, drawing on the energy and expertise of a diverse range of citizens.

In northern Pakistan, WWF and its partners are working with poor communities to reduce conflicts that are resulting in deforestation, erosion and loss of economically valuable trees. In Madagascar, WWF is helping develop an integrated approach to primary health care, through promoting the use of local plants in traditional remedies. And in the Brazilian Amazon, WWF is supporting efforts by villagers to harvest sustainably their freshwater fisheries. These are examples of the programme to reconcile the development needs of local communities with the conservation of their resources that WWF is now delivering in more than 70 countries around the world.

But it is not only in poorer countries that community involvement in sustainable development is important. For example, WWF is working with local authorities and neighbourhood groups in Reading, UK, to support their Local Agenda 21 process. At the neighbourhood level, people's aspirations for an improved quality of life encompass the local environment as well as global issues. Sustainability means taking action on saving energy, minimising waste, creating community gardens, cleaning up rivers, improving access to social services and encouraging alternatives to use of private cars.

The impact of such decentralised, micro-level initiatives is growing. Yet too often, short-sighted and inappropriate policies at the regional and national level undermine rather than encourage imaginative local initiatives. There has been a widespread failure of governments to respond to the challenge of a sustainable future. Local action relies on a supportive framework of public policies. These must devolve decision-making to the appropriate level, support education for sustainable development, establish the right economic incentives, and provide public resources for social and environmental services that the market cannot deliver. Creating this framework is a major challenge. But, at the local, national and international level, it is one which can be met.

tainable' environmental limits; the need to integrate environmental and economic policy; the requirement to take explicit political account of the future, and to adapt government institutions to new conditions of complexity and uncertainty; the link between environmental degradation and poverty – are the central themes underlying the concept of 'sustainable development' (see Panel 4). Since the Rio Earth Summit in 1992, sustainable development has been endorsed as a policy objective by virtually every

Panel 4

Sustainable Development

The concept of sustainable development was first popularised by the Brundtland Report, *Our Common Future* (1987), which defined it as 'development which meets the needs of the present without compromising the ability of future generations to meet their own needs.' A second definition, also now widely used, was given by the United Nations Environment Programme / World Wide Fund for Nature / World Conservation Union Report *Caring for the Earth* (1991): 'Improving the quality of life while living within the carrying capacity of supporting ecosystems'.

Although there are differing interpretations of what sustainable development requires in practice, the term has been very widely adopted, reflecting the understanding that economic development cannot go on degrading the environment indefinitely. The core meanings of the term now have wide agreement. They are that the environment must be protected in such a way as to preserve essential ecosystem functions and to provide for the wellbeing of future generations; that environmental and economic policy must be integrated; that the goal of policy should be an improvement in the overall quality of life, not just income growth; that poverty must be ended and resources distributed more equally; and that all sections of society must be involved in decision making.

The goal of sustainable development was endorsed by 149 countries (including the UK) at the United Nations 'Earth Summit' in Rio de Janeiro in 1992. The conference agreed a global action plan for sustainable development, *Agenda* 21. Countries were asked to draw up national sustainable development plans and to report on them to the UN Commission on Sustainable Development. The UK produced its Strategy in 1994. 'Local Agenda 21s' for sustainable development are now being drawn up in many towns, cities and regions in Britain and throughout the world (See Witness Box 23 on p113).

Sources: World Commission on Environment and Development, *Our Common Future* (Oxford: Oxford University Press, 1987); *Caring for the Earth* (London: Earthscan UNEP, WWF, IUCN, 1991).

country in the world, including the UK. But as the British Government's own National Sustainable Development Strategy starkly revealed,[9] rhetorical commitment has not been matched by necessary action.

Addressing the environmental crisis will require both national and international efforts to change the direction of economic development. The key elements of the problem can be expressed in the relationships between three factors: per capita consumption, population growth, and the 'productivity' with which the environment is used. Something of the scale of the issues can then be represented by the 'sustainability equation' (see Panel 5).

Panel 5

The Sustainability Equation

The relationship between environmental impact and human activity can be expressed in the equation $I = P \times C \times T$, where

I = environmental impact
P = population
C = consumption per person
T = environmental impact per unit of consumption: that is, a measure of how efficiently the economy uses natural resources and produces wastes.

Very simple calculations can be used to show the order of magnitude of the improvements in the efficiency of resource use and waste production, T, required to achieve significant reductions in environmental impact, I.

For example, let us say that human impact on the environment needs to be reduced by 50% over the next 50 years. Let us also assume that the world economy grows by 2–3% per annum, which implies a quadrupling of consumption (C) by 2050, and that world population (P) doubles over the next fifty years. Then T would have to be one-sixteenth its current level by the year 2050. In other words, technologies and living patterns would have to be 91% more environmentally efficient then than they are now. This may or may not be possible. It will certainly not happen without deliberate policy intervention.

It is important to recognise that the root of the problem lies in the industrialised countries. Although only 9% of projected global population growth will occur in the North, consumption in rich countries is so much more than in the South that the extra projected 60 million Northerners will be responsible for more environmental degradation than the 900 million additional people who will live in poorer countries. Sinxe living standards must rise in the South, the improvement in environmental efficiency in the North will probably have to be greater than 91%. (See Panel 8 on p31.)

Improving T does not just mean improving technology, conventionally understood. T can be reduced by different ways of organising economic life (eg by reducing travel distances), and by new consumption patterns (eg shifting demand from high-impact consumer goods to low-impact services). I can also fall if consumption itself is reduced.

Sources: P Ekins and M Jacobs, 'Environmental Sustainability and the Growth of GDP: Conditions for Compatibility', in V Bhaskar and A Glyn (eds), *The North, The South and the Environment* (London: Earthscan, 1995), and P Harrison, *The Third Revolution: Population, Environment and a Sustainable World* (London: Penguin, 1993).

While population growth on its own is not responsible for environmental degradation, it inevitably increases pressure on the natural environment. In the large industrialising countries (such as China, India and Brazil) such growth compounds the burden caused by rising consumption.

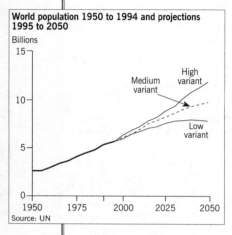

World population 1950 to 1994 and projections 1995 to 2050

Billions

In mid-1995 the population of the world was estimated as 5.7 billion. It will be six billion by 1998. Although overall fertility rates have fallen, population growth continues at around 1.57% pa, or 94 million additional people every year. The United Nations has made three alternative projections for population growth in the future. The 'medium' projection assumes that fertility will continue to decline. Global population will then reach 8.3 billion by the year 2025 and 9.8 billion by 2050. If fertility rates do not decline (the 'high variant'), the total is projected to be 11.9 billion in 2050. But if the measures agreed at the UN Cairo Conference on Population and Development in 1994 are implemented, population growth would be much slower. The 'low' projection results in a population of 7.9 billion in 2050. The difference between the low and medium scenarios is 1.9 billion, and between low and high, 4.0 billion – that is, equal to the entire world population in 1974.

Source: United Nations, *World Population Prospects: The 1994 Revision* (New York: UN, 1995); United Nations Population Fund, *The State of the World Population* 1994 (New York: UNFPA, 1994).

Within the space of a generation, for example, China's present rate of combined population and economic growth will make it the largest economy in the world. With a per capita consumption level similar to that now enjoyed by South Korea, its carbon dioxide emissions will exceed those of all today's industrialised nations put together.[10] Meanwhile, population growth among the world's poorest peoples often adds to the stresses on the already degraded environments, both rural and urban, in which they live. Rapid population growth is both a cause and a consequence of poverty.

The means to slow population growth, however, are now known and available. At the Cairo Conference on Population and Development in September 1994 the world's governments agreed a Programme of Action reflecting the experience of those countries and regions where population

> ## Witness Box 2
>
> ### **Population and Women's Lives**
> #### By *Population Concern*
>
> Most women in the UK take it for granted that they can exercise self-determination in their reproductive lives. But in less developed countries an estimated 350 million women and their partners still lack access to a full range of modern family planning information and services. Roughly 28 per cent of all pregnancies worldwide end in abortion and many more are unplanned and mistimed.
>
> The implications of a woman's ability to determine the timing and spacing of her childbearing are not just personal. Where women can choose to plan their families, there are benefits to their own health and equality of opportunity, to the wellbeing and education of their children, and to the conservation of the environment and resources.
>
> We know that where services are made available in a way which is culturally sensitive, women want them. Only 21 months after the launch of a Population Concern programme in the Sidamo region of Ethiopia, modern contraceptive use in the region had shown a five-fold increase. At the moment only 3 per cent of women in Ethiopia as a whole are using modern methods of family planning. The comparative figure for use of modern methods of family planning by women in the UK is 71 per cent. Poverty is not only defined by income, but by lack of choices. Women suffer disproportionately from both: they represent 70 per cent of the world's poor and two-thirds of those who are illiterate.
>
> If every woman had access to the services she wanted to plan her family the world would be on its way to achieving a slower population increase, in the region of the United Nations 'Low' Projection of 7.9 billion in 2050. The difference between the Low and High projections is 4 billion. It would cost an estimated $10.2 billion per year to meet the family planning aspirations of the entire world's people. Developing countries themselves will be trying to provide two-thirds of this money. UNICEF argue that 'Family planning could bring more benefits to more people at less cost than any other single technology now available to the human race.' By equipping women and men to take charge of their reproductive health we can make our contribution to safeguarding the wellbeing of both people and planet.

growth has been reduced. It encompasses a variety of complementary measures. First is the emancipation of and provision of education for women: everywhere in the world, women with higher status and more opportunity have fewer children. The availability of family planning education and the provision of family planning services are then crucial to make smaller families possible. At the same time improving child health care and increasing incomes and economic security make larger families less necessary.[11] (See Witness Box 2.)

Panel 7

Ecological Footprints

Goods and services which are bought in the UK do not only have an impact on the environment in the UK. They also affect environments elsewhere. Some impacts are global, such as those of carbon dioxide emissions (causing the greenhouse effect) and CFCs and HCFCs (depleting the ozone layer). Others are regional: acid rain produced by British power stations causes damage to forests and lakes in Scandinavia. Many of the UK's environmental impacts occur in the particular countries from which we import.

For example, large-scale cotton production for export causes severe environmental damage in low-income nations such as India, China, Pakistan, Paraguay and the countries of the Sahel in West Africa. The damage includes wildlife loss and human ill-health from pesticide poisoning (worldwide, cotton accounts for 25% of all pesticide consumption); salinisation and water depletion from over-irrigation; soil erosion resulting from the displacement of pasture land; and pollution from textile manufacture. A proportion of this damage can be attributed to demand for cotton coming from the UK.

Impacts such as these which occur elsewhere are sometimes described as a country's 'ecological footprint': the impression left behind by our consumption patterns. Reducing the UK's ecological footprint is an important aspect of sustainability: improving our own environment is not enough if we are simultaneously degrading other people's.

Sources: N Robins (ed), *Citizen Action to Lighten Britain's Ecological Footprints: A Report to the Department of Environment* (London: International Institute for Environment and Development, 1995). Ecological footprints are further explored and measured in M Wackernagel and W Rees, *Our Ecological Footprint: Reducing Human Impact on the Earth* (Gabriola Island, BC: New Society, 1995)

The Cairo Programme represents a landmark in the linking of policy on population growth, women's rights and development. If fully implemented – at an annual cost equivalent to about 3 per cent of the world's arms spending – it would lead to a global population in 2050 of approximately 7.9 billion instead of 11.9 billion.[12] The benefits this would bring, to the lives of the world's poorest women and families, and to the global environment, make its implementation a matter of the highest international priority.

Yet population growth is only half the issue. It's the one upon which Northern governments and media generally focus; but that's because they wish to avoid the other, more uncomfortable figures in the sustainability equation. Global environmental degradation is not primarily caused by those countries in which population is rising most rapidly. With just 20 per cent of the world's people, the industrialised countries are responsible for three

Sustainable Consumption:

The Concept of Environmental Space

What would a sustainable level of consumption be? Two factors are involved. The first is the earth's 'carrying capacity': the maximum harvest of renewable resources such as timber and fish which can be sustained without depleting the stock; the total area of productive land available for agriculture; the maximum rate at which the atmosphere can absorb carbon dioxide without causing long-term global warming; the maximum rate of environmental assimilation of other wastes and pollutants; and so on. The second factor concerns the *distribution* of this carrying capacity. Which people on the earth are to use its resources? At present the distribution is very unequal: 80–90% of environmental capacities are consumed by the 20% of the global population who live in industrialised countries. If living standards in the South are to rise, the earth's resources will have to be more equally shared between the world's people.

Through a combination of scientific and political judgements, it is possible to estimate current global carrying capacity. (In some cases, by raising the productivity of the natural environment, it may be possible to increase this.) If this is then divided by the global population, a figure for per capita carrying capacity can be calculated. This is each person's *environmental space*: the amount of environmental consumption we would each be allowed if the sustainable global total were shared out equally. This figure can then be compared to our actual consumption of environmental resources. The difference is the *unsustainability gap*: the amount by which current consumption exceeds available space. This gap is a measure not just of environmental unsustainability but of inequity: of the maldistribution of the world's resources.

In a study for Friends of the Earth Europe, the Wuppertal Institute has calculated the approximate environmental space available for a number of environmental resources and waste assimilation capacities. It has then compared these with present European consumption levels. To achieve sustainability while allowing room for higher living standards in the South, the Institute shows that significant reductions in European consumption will be required. Since such reductions cannot be achieved immediately, the Institute suggests interim 'sustainability targets' for 2010 which make feasible progress towards the sustainable level.

Resource	Present use per capita pa	Environmental space per capita pa	Change needed	Target 2010
CO_2 emissions	7.3t	1.7t	−77%	5.4t(−26%)
Cement	536 kg	80 kg	−85%	423 kg(−21%)
Aluminium	12 kg	1.2 kg	−90%	9.2 kg (−23%)
Chlorine	23 kg	0 kg	−100%	17.2 kg (−25%)
Wood	0.66 m³	0.56 m³	−15%	0.56 m³ (−15%)

The target reductions are technologically and socially feasible, but they will require active policy interventions, and almost certainly changes in lifestyles.

Source: Friends of the Earth Europe, *Towards Sustainable Europe* (Brussels: FoE Europe, 1995).

quarters of the world's energy consumption (two-thirds of all greenhouse gases), 80 per cent of its iron and steel use, 93 per cent of global industrial effluents and 95 per cent of hazardous waste. The average British citizen consumes approximately 20 times the environmental resources of the average Indian, and more than 200 times that of a person born in one of the least developed nations of sub-Saharan Africa.[13] Even in the South itself, deforestation, the depletion of marine stocks and industrial pollution are substantially the result of Northern, not Southern, demand. (See Panel 7.)

In a world of environmental limits, this inequality of environmental consumption makes the Northern injunction that the South should reduce its environmental impacts both hypocritical and ineffective. As global communications increase, so do aspirations to Northern lifestyles. It will be quite impossible to persuade Southern governments, let alone their peoples, that such aspirations are wrong and that policies to realise them should be abandoned. The only hope of reducing the impact of the South upon the global environment will be to change the patterns of Northern consumption first. (See Panel 8.)

Such an objective is commonly regarded as self-sacrificial, its motivation altruistic. But this is very odd. If, in aiming for current Northern consumption levels, the large industrialising countries of the South follow similar development paths, the world's environment will be simply overwhelmed. Bringing Southern energy consumption to the present levels of industrialised countries, for example, would involve a ten-fold increase in the global total. The Intergovernmental Panel on Climate Change suggests that global warming demands a reduction in fossil fuel use by as much as 50 per cent.[14] Generalised global industrialisation on the current Northern model would bring catastrophic pollution, resource depletion, land degradation and biodiversity loss, affecting the living patterns, security and stability of every Northern nation. It is this prospect which would better merit the description of self-sacrifice. Altruism would not seem to be a necessary motivation for avoiding it.

Economic Growth and Quality of Life

Yet this still leaves a large question unanswered. Would not changing Northern consumption patterns involve a drastic reduction in living standards? If so, it would hardly seem to represent a feasible politics for any foreseeable government, in Britain or anywhere else.

The crucial relationship, unsurprisingly, is between environmental degradation and economic growth. Reducing the economy's impact on the environment will require improvements in resource efficiency: that is, in the rate at which resources are consumed and pollution generated per unit of output. Investments will have to be made in new technologies and new production and distribution systems: these will have to be more energy efficient, less wasteful and less polluting ('cleaner') than those they replace. New patterns of living will be required involving shorter and fewer daily journeys, more use of public transport, greater reuse and recycling of materials, longer lasting products and more energy efficient consumption.

But such changes will not, as once feared, call growth to a halt. On the contrary, the evidence suggests that the reverse may be the case.[15] Some environmental measures may have growth-retarding effects, as investment spending is diverted from more 'productive' uses. But much of the investment will itself be stimulatory, creating jobs directly and through multiplier effects, and encouraging innovation. Since energy consumption and waste cost money, reducing them may raise general productivity. Countries which act quickly may gain 'first mover' competitive advantage in the new technologies, winning overseas market shares. Particular bene-fits seem likely from the 'ecological' reform of the tax system, shifting the burden of taxation away from labour and VAT, towards energy, transport and waste. (This is discussed further below.) In these ways environmental policies offer considerable opportunities for job creation (see Panel 9). There are obviously crucial riders here, such as whether measures are intro-duced in Britain alone or more widely, but the fear that economic growth and competitiveness would of necessity collapse under the environmental imperative is evidently misplaced.

This does not mean, however, that average disposable incomes would rise. A more sustainable economy would have higher investment; it is unlikely to have higher private consumption. Where additional consump-tion is required it will often have to be in the public sector, on goods such as public transport, environmental protection, health care and education. Moreover, as we discuss in Chapter 5, social justice requires a redistribu-

Jobs, Economic Performance and Environmental Policy

A common argument used against stronger environmental policies is that they tend to retard economic performance and destroy jobs. But this need not be the case; indeed the evidence suggests that environmental policy tends in general to create jobs.

In nearly all the studies conducted for the OECD, European Commission and national governments, environmental policies have been shown either to be neutral in their economic effects or slightly to raise output and employment. They tend to have little impact on competitiveness, particularly if introduced at a European level; other factors, such as exchange rate fluctuations and labour costs, are much more important.

These benign effects occur because environmental policies tend to stimulate investment. To meet higher environmental standards firms must install energy efficient and 'clean' technologies, engage in waste minimisation, develop new products, improve their environmental management, and so on. This investment raises costs, but it also increases output and employment in the firms which make and supply the new environmental goods and services. The 'environmental sector' is now very large: globally the OECD estimates it at $200bn (larger than the aerospace industry) rising to $300bn in 2000. Britain's environmental sector already employs over 100,000 people.

The countries with the largest environmental sectors – where job creation has been most significant – are those with the strongest environmental policy: Japan, the US, Germany, Sweden. High domestic standards have bred technological innovation as firms find ways of meeting them at lowest cost. This has then led to the development of export-oriented environmental sectors, creating new jobs, as the leading firms gain a 'first mover advantage' in overseas markets.

The potential for job creation from environmental policy in the UK is very significant. It is estimated that a ten-year national domestic energy conservation programme could create 500,000 job years (ie 50,000 jobs lasting ten years each) at a cost of just £23,000 per job. Much of this expenditure could be paid for through reduced fuel bills. Not only would this tackle fuel poverty; the jobs would be located in areas where unemployment is highest. Friends of the Earth estimate that up to 10,000 additional jobs could be created from investment in wind and solar power over a ten year period; approximately 15,000 from shifting public expenditure from roads to railways; over 20,000 from increased recycling of waste materials; 80,000 from stronger pollution control policies; and 12–18,000 from a movement towards organic agriculture. Many of these new jobs, along with others caused by multiplier effects, could be stimulated by an 'ecological' reform of the taxation system. This is discussed further in Panel 20 on pp94.

Sources: OECD, *Environmental Policies and International Competitiveness* (Paris: OECD, 1993); ECOTEC, *The Potential for Employment Opportunities from Pursuing Sustainable Development* (Dublin: European Foundation for the Improvement of Living and Working Conditions, 1994); M Jacobs, *Green Jobs? The Employment Implications of Environmental Policy* (Brussels: World Wide Fund for Nature, 1994); Friends of the Earth, *Working Future? Jobs and the Environment* (London: FoE, 1994).

tion of national income towards the poor. It cannot therefore be expected that the disposable incomes of ordinary, reasonably comfortable households in Britain will rise significantly year on year as the political system has come to expect. There is no reason for them to fall; but sustainability probably does mean that the era of taken-for-granted exponential consumption growth is at an end.

We do not believe, however, that this would be the catastrophe commonly predicted. As many people have realised over recent years (if only by default), consumption of public goods can make a higher contribution to wellbeing than equivalent spending on private goods. Ensuring environmental sustainability offers particular gains for 'quality of life' – and not simply through the long-term expectation of living in a reasonably stable, functioning world. Pollution, in its myriad forms, causes serious ill-health. Traffic congestion adds to the unproductive travelling time which takes up so much of modern life, and makes urban living stressful and dangerous, particularly for children. The destruction of the countryside and natural habitats robs us of pleasure in the beauty, complexity and tranquillity of the natural world, and detaches people from their physical roots and their sense of belonging to particular places. Other kinds of environmental damage require us to spend vast sums on protective measures – from flood barriers to sun creams – which could be devoted to more useful things.

For these reasons, we believe, sustainability is compatible with improved, not reduced living standards. The definition of living standards would have to change – we could no longer assume that private disposable income measured them. We would have to include also those contributions to wellbeing which were provided free by nature, or secured by public action, paid for through taxation. Some expectations of life would no doubt have to change. But the claim is reasonably confident: a sustainable economy would make us better off, not worse. We shall return to this in Chapter 5.

Sustainability Policy

Can sustainability be implemented? The instruments themselves are straightforward and familiar: regulatory standards for emissions and energy efficiency; financial incentives such as pollution charges and recycling

---

Witness Box 3

Moving On
By *Transport* 2000

From the moment we step out of the door, transport has an impact on our lives.

Traffic congestion, roads destroying countryside and towns, declining bus and rail services, 3600 road deaths and 300,000 serious injuries a year, pollution which severely harms human health, emissions which add to global warming... These are just some of the problems resulting from current transport policies.

As public transport has declined, so car use has increased. The whole shape of our towns and cities has changed, with shops, workplaces, even hospitals, planned around the car. Yet a third of all households have no car; many people are increasingly isolated and effectively denied access to facilities. Almost half of all journeys are under two miles. These journeys – to the park, to the shops, to pick up the kids from school – are ideal for walking and cycling. But for many people, there is too much traffic on the roads for this healthy way of travelling to feel safe and enjoyable.

We can cut traffic if the alternatives to cars and lorries are improved. First, we must reduce the need to travel by car. This means promoting development which can be reached easily on foot, by bike or public transport. Road building which simply generates more traffic should be stopped.

Second, investment in public transport should be increased, to provide cheap, reliable, fast and frequent public transport, making it a real alternative to the car. This would include coordinated local bus and rail services, bus priority measures, urban light rail systems and fully accessible buses and trains. Distortions in the tax system which encourage unnecessary journeys by car, such as company car tax relief, should be ended.

Third, we must reclaim the streets for people. Parking controls, reduced speed limits, cycling facilities and traffic bans can all help.

Such programmes can largely be paid for if existing transport spending is re-allocated. Reducing the car culture and car dependency is not so much a question of money as of political will.

---

rebates; land use planning and public expenditures on infrastructure; the use of civil liability law and consumer education; government support for research and development and for industrial restructuring; changes to the culture and regulation of financial institutions to encourage a longer-term investment perspective. Some of the required measures will no doubt be politically difficult at first, for example in the field of transport. Reducing the proportion of urban and long-distance journeys made by cars and lorries will require a patient and careful mixture of disincentive sticks, public

Farming, Food and Folly

By the SAFE Alliance (Sustainable Agriculture,
Food and Environment Alliance)

Many of the social and environmental problems affecting rural areas are interlinked. Rural services decline – meaning fewer schools, shops and post offices, and worse public transport – as farming intensifies and sheds labour. More specialisation requires more inputs, like imported animal feeds and energy-intensive agro chemicals. As mixed farming disappears, with it goes diversity in the landscape, and traditional land uses like orchards, hop and hay fields and coppice woodland.

Through the European Common Agricultural Policy, the UK spends £3 billion on UK farming, including nearly £1 billion in direct compensation to farmers for losing subsidies previously linked to food prices. In return for this support they have been obliged to set some land aside or reduce animal stocking rates as a measure to reduce food production. Meanwhile environmental spending on agriculture is well below £100 million, or less than 4 per cent of the total; farms get even larger; and UK farm employment falls further below any comparable country. Organic agriculture, which represents the best practice in sustainable farming by using natural systems rather than chemical methods, receives only £1 million per annum in incentives for conventional farmers to convert. Yet almost 70 per cent of organic food eaten in the UK is imported, most of it from countries with similar climatic conditions.

It need not be like this. Beneficial policies can work. Even within the CAP other European countries are maintaining farm employment, enhancing the countryside, and producing food which consumers want to buy. Assistance for organic farmers is consistently shown to be popular with the public – in stark contrast to existing policies. More organic and low-input farming would also begin to address other concerns – like animal welfare, over-production, the decline in farmland birds and other wildlife, contamination of food with harmful pesticide residues and, through more direct marketing, the excessive and unnecessary transport of food. Targetting support to those who really need it, such as hill and smaller farmers, would help maintain a diverse and viable farm community across the UK. By addressing public concerns in an integrated way, these measures could have the added attraction of saving money.

transport carrots, measures to make cycling and walking safer, and public persuasion (see Witness Box 3). But experience on the continent shows that such a reduction is eminently possible, and there is increasing evidence of popular support for the required measures.[16] Reform in other areas of policy, from energy to agriculture, will take similar boldness; but in few cases is lack of practicality the barrier to implementation.[17]

One particular field of policy is generating considerable interest now throughout Europe. This is the idea of 'eco-tax reform': raising taxes on energy consumption, transport and waste, while reducing them on VAT and labour (in the UK, employers' National Insurance Contributions). As a fiscally neutral overall package, eco-tax reform appears to offer a 'triple dividend'. It will lead to significant reductions in environmental impact, substantial increases in employment, and greater general efficiency in the economy as the disincentive effects of existing taxes are reduced. We discuss this further in the context of employment policy in Chapter 5.

Interestingly, industry is not as opposed to environmental policy as is commonly thought. Successive reports from the Government's own Advisory Committee on Business and the Environment – and also recently from the Confederation of British Industry – have confirmed this.[18] While there should be no illusions about the obstacles likely to be encountered, most large companies have now recognised that rising environmental costs (for example, in transport congestion) can only be controlled by public policy. They argue that voluntary measures are unlikely to be effective, since companies with high environmental standards are liable to be undercut by those without; ensuring a level playing field through effective enforcement is crucial. Indeed, much of industry now accepts that the severity of environmental standards is not the main issue. Rather, it is the flexibility which companies are given in meeting such standards, and the certainty which the regulatory framework provides over the medium term. If clear performance targets are set which allow firms to innovate, and timetables for compliance are reasonable, most industries can improve their environmental performance. Moreover, the commercial gains to be made from environmental product innovation and new, more efficient investment are also considerable, and have not passed unnoticed.[19] (See Panel 9.)

What all of this presupposes, of course, is that governments may legitimately intervene in the economy to achieve socially-determined ends where market forces otherwise fail. This is not the belief which has informed economic policy in Britain in recent years. But it is surely inescapable. Market forces will not generate sustainability of their own accord. Driven by short-term competition, they tend to provide insufficient investment in public goods; they are prone to generate external costs; and they generally under-value or 'discount' the future. Markets can of course be used to stimulate and achieve environmental efficiency – this is precisely the purpose of financial incentives and the eco-tax reform. But sustainability is ultimately a political choice, and it will require proactive government policy to achieve it.

Moreover, this will be true not just on a national scale, but internationally (and regionally and locally too). As is already the case, many of the instruments will be best introduced, perhaps indeed only properly effective, at a European level. Ultimately, some will require international treaties – not an easy prospect, but one which the Montreal Protocol on CFCs and the ozone layer shows is possible. As we shall argue in the next chapter, controlling the overseas environmental impacts of Northern economies will also require regulations on trade. Again, there is no shirking the difficulties involved. But the alternatives are worse; and the difficulties are surmountable. The functioning of the natural environment provides the physical context and economic base for all human activities. If we do not meet this challenge – and we have, on authoritative estimates, perhaps 35–40 years to reverse the trends of the last 200[20] – most of the others we face will surely prove impossible.

Only Connect...
From Global Poverty to International Security

Making the Links

After three decades of 'development', the facts of global poverty represent a shocking measure of failure. 1.3 billion people, more than a fifth of the human race, live in absolute poverty, lacking access to basic necessities such as food and clean drinking water. One-third of the world's children are undernourished, and 12.2 million die before the age of five every year, 95 per cent of them from poverty-related illnesses. Half the world's population lacks regular access to the most essential drugs, and 900 million people are illiterate. Population growth means that most of these are larger absolute numbers than 25 years ago.[1] Since the early 1960s average real per capita income in industrialised countries has more than doubled. In South Asia, starting from a base 40 times lower, it has risen by 80 per cent; in Latin America and the Caribbean, by only 50 per cent. In sub-Saharan Africa per capita income has not risen at all.[2]

Such figures must be set against important gains. Many countries have experienced substantial increases in national income and significant improvements in standards of nutrition, literacy, health care and sanitation. Several of the newly industrialising countries of East Asia and Latin America enjoy industrial output and urban middle class living standards comparable to parts of the developed world. There can be little question that, for particular sections of the populations of these countries, the promise of 'development' has indeed been realised.

The problem is that the fruits of such development have been extremely unequally shared. Sub-Saharan Africa has barely shared in them at all: alone among the major regions of the world, the proportion of the population living in poverty is forecast to rise in the period from 1985 to

Global Poverty and Inequality

The first figure below shows World Bank data and projections for the percentage of the population of different regions of the world living below the poverty line. The absolute numbers of the poor are also given. The 'poverty line' is extremely low, defined as an annual per capita income of $370 (1985 dollars). Despite economic growth, no decline in poverty is expected in this period in sub-Saharan Africa, in Latin America and the Caribbean, and in North Africa and the Middle East. In fact the more or less constant percentages disguise the fact that, because of population growth, the absolute number of people living in poverty in these regions is rising.

Percentage of population below the poverty line and absolute numbers of poor people

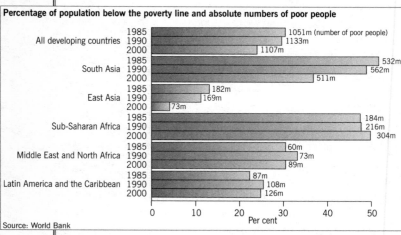

Source: World Bank

The second figure shows the ratio of income shares in the world economy. The gap between the richest 20% of the world's population and the poorest 20% has more than doubled in the last thirty years. 85% of world income now goes to the richest 20%, up from 70% in 1960. The share of the poorest 20% has fallen from 2.3% to 1.4%.

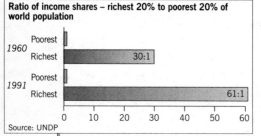

These figures show not only the extent of poverty in the world, but the widening inequality between the world's richest and poorest people. Despite world economic growth, and improvements in some regions, poverty as a whole is not being reduced.

Sources: World Bank, *World Development Report* 1992 (Washington: World Bank, 1992); UN Development Programme, *Human Development Report* 1994 (Oxford: Oxford University Press, 1994).

2000.[3] (See Panel 10.) In other countries, particularly in Latin America, rising wealth among the middle and upper classes has been accompanied by an increase in the numbers of the poor and a drastic fall in their living standards.[4] In almost every country of the South, women bear the greatest burden of poverty, subject to lower incomes, worse health, worse educational levels and longer working hours than men.[5]

It is this growing inequality, both within and between countries, which is the new face of the Third World. It changes the nature of old arguments.

Once upon a time, it might have looked as if only history and charity connected us to the developing countries. As the material affluence of Western societies increased, it was certainly difficult to justify the persistence of absolute poverty and hunger in the Third World, particularly for countries such as Britain whose colonial regimes were clearly implicated. But comfort could be gained from the expectation of the future. The moral affront was temporary: as economic growth and development spread, they would gradually eliminate the spectre of malnutrition, preventable disease and urban squalor. In the meantime, the charitable impulse – manifested through national aid policies and private donation – seemed to express our connection with the world's poor.

If this picture was ever valid, it is not now, for three reasons. First, it can no longer be argued that the pursuit of development based on economic growth will eliminate poverty. On the contrary, as we shall show below, it has become increasingly apparent that the existing processes of economic development cause poverty even as they generate wealth. Recognising this then revises the ethical case. Human suffering and injustice can no longer be tolerated on the grounds that 'progress' will gradually eliminate them. General aid for economic growth is now morally inadequate. It has become imperative rather for the rich nations to tackle poverty directly, in particular by addressing those aspects of their own international economic policy which contribute to it.

Second, it is evident that what happens in the South cannot be roped off from the experience of Northern societies. Increasing poverty, allied to increasing environmental degradation, is generating new fields of conflict and tension, and creating ever larger numbers of refugees and migrants. This cannot be confined to individual countries and regions; it spills over into the international arena, where the security and stability of rich countries are inevitably affected. As the Brandt Report insisted nearly 20 years ago, poverty reduction is in our interest too.[6]

Third, the common forces which create wealth and poverty are international as well as national. This means that the processes of development in the North and in the South are not independent. We cannot – as once seemed possible – have our economic growth in the UK and worry separately about what is happening in the Third World. What is happening there is part of what happens in Britain. Trade, investment and employment patterns in this country are intimately bound up with such patterns in the South, for they are governed by the same international corporations and market forces.

The relationship between North and South has therefore changed. Desperate and widespread poverty, reflecting gross inequality in the life chances of rich and poor, remains ethically intolerable. But this is not the limit of the connection between countries such as the UK and those of the Third World. The closer ties of a smaller planet and a global economy have other effects. They make concern about what happens there more than charity.

Economic Globalisation, Free Trade and Poverty

More than ever before, we live today in a global economy. Trade in goods and services, flows of capital and investment, and the activities of huge transnational corporations increasingly cross national borders, linking peoples to one another in industrialised and developing countries alike. (See Panel 11.) This process of globalisation has been strongly encouraged by international economic policy. Capital flows have been deregulated throughout the world. The belief that the liberalisation of trade is beneficial to all countries has been the driving force behind regional trade agreements such as the European Single Market and the North American Free Trade Agreement (NAFTA), and the emerging trade blocs of the Asia-Pacific rim (APEC) and Latin America (Mercosur). On a global scale it has underpinned the development of the General Agreement on Tariffs and Trade (GATT), particularly through the Uruguay Round finally completed in 1994, and the consequent creation of the World Trade Organisation (WTO). The same belief motivates the national policies adopted by the International Monetary Fund (IMF) and World Bank in their 'structural adjustment' programmes of assistance to developing countries.

Panel 11

Globalisation

The term 'globalisation' refers to the growing integration of the world economy and the increasingly international reach of modern communications.

During the post-war period world trade has grown twelve-fold. This is much faster than output growth (which has grown by five times), so that in most countries imports and exports make up a much larger proportion of economic activity than before. International trade flows now amount to over $4 trillion pa. Trade has increased not just between industrialised countries, but between North and South. The same is true of foreign investment. Although by far the largest proportion of capital movements occur between industrialised countries, private investment flows from industrialised to developing countries grew by a factor of twenty between 1970 and 1992 (from $5 billion to $102 billion). At the same time the total external debt of the developing world rose fifteen-fold (from $100 billion to $1,500 billion).

The expansion of global trade and the increasing mobility of capital is reflected in the growth of transnational corporations (TNCs) and the 'internationalisation' of production. Two thirds of world trade is now accounted for by just 500 companies, and 40% of it occurs *within* these companies. Some of these companies are very large indeed: the ten largest – including corporations such as General Motors, Ford, Exxon and Shell – have a gross income greater than the GNP of 100 of the world's poorest countries. Though originating mainly in the US, Europe and Japan, TNCs are increasingly organising their production on a globally coordinated basis.

Globalisation has been powerfully stimulated by the deregulation of capital flows, with the fastest international integration occuring in the financial system. It has been made possible by the development of new information technologies, which allow for rapid international financial transactions and enable production systems to become more flexible. At the same time trade rules have been liberalised. These tendencies have reinforced one another, as increasingly severe international competition drives firms to cut costs. At the same time, the expansion of television and product brand names has created an increasingly 'global' culture – from McDonalds to Michael Jackson.

The extent of globalisation should not be exaggerated, however. It does not mean that distinctively national economies no longer exist, and therefore that national economic policy is no longer effective. Much of domestic output and employment – particularly in services – is still subject mainly to domestic demand. Different countries retain distinctively national economic institutions and investment cultures. For example, the Japanese form of coordinated government–corporate planning, and the close connections between German banks and industry, each make for an economic system very different from that of the UK. What it does mean is that national economies are more vulnerable to economic changes occurring in other parts of the world than they used to be (for example, banking crises and currency speculation) and that individual countries no longer have effective sovereignty over particular areas of economic policy. In turn this means that in these areas (where capital flows and trade are affected) eco-

The argument is that freer trade – the reduction of tariff and non-tariff barriers – increases competition, raises efficiency and thereby releases resources for productive growth. Increasing capital mobility encourages investment to flow to where it will create most wealth. At a national level, 'structural adjustment' seeks to support these processes by reducing public spending, deregulating markets and encouraging export-oriented agriculture.

For certain countries, and for particular social groups within them, integration into the global economy has brought considerable benefits. The success of the first wave of newly industrialising countries in East Asia – South Korea, Hong Kong, Taiwan, Singapore – is now well known. By diversifying out of agriculture and primary production into manufacturing, these countries have experienced rapid economic growth (more than 7 per cent a year on average for the last three decades) and have made major inroads into poverty. In the last decade a second wave of industrialisation has taken off, in countries such as China, Malaysia, Thailand, Mexico, Brazil and Chile. This has been led by direct foreign investment, attracted by low costs and low taxation. Again, rapid economic growth has resulted, generating significant improvement in urban middle class living standards.[7]

But unfortunately these cases do not tell the full story, and they do not prove that the trade liberalisation/structural adjustment model of globalisation can eliminate poverty or bring about generalised social development. On the contrary, in the vast majority of Third World countries, and for the poor in many of the newly industrialising ones themselves, integration into the global economy has exacerbated poverty, particularly for women. It has made the meeting of basic needs more difficult, not less.

It is crucial to recognise that the East Asian experience cannot be used to support the trade-liberalisation model of global integration for the rest of the developing world. In the first place – this is too often forgotten

– the original 'tiger' economies have not pursued policies of free trade. With the exception of Hong Kong, in each of these countries diversification has been actively pursued through state economic planning and intervention, and been protected by tariff and non-tariff barriers to imports. Strict conditions have been imposed on foreign investment, including rigid exchange controls.[8]

Supported in most cases by expatriate Chinese capital and substantial aid from the West, the East Asian economies were able to specialise in fast-growing, high-value-added manufacturing sectors. Without these advantages, the majority of countries in sub-Saharan Africa, Latin America, the Caribbean and the rest of Asia have had to specialise in primary commodities. World trade in commodities has been much slower, and prices have been falling for two decades – while the prices of manufactured imports have consistently risen. For many years these circumstances were exacerbated by the policies of many African governments, whose high taxation and over-valued exchange rates penalised producers and systematically undermined their world market shares.

Moreover, attempts to diversify into higher value added sectors such as commodity processing and manufacturing have consistently run up against tariffs and quotas imposed by industrialised countries. Such protectionism gives the lie to the idea that Britain and its European partners have really been committed to 'free trade'. Many of these restrictions will be gradually reduced under the terms of the GATT agreement, but they will not be eliminated. At the same time, developing countries will have to open up strategic sectors of their economies to international competition. Without countervailing measures, the main beneficiaries of such a liberalisation will be in the North. Meanwhile, the GATT agreement will not prevent continued dumping of EU and US agricultural surpluses on world markets, which has critically undermined domestic food production in much of Africa and Latin America. In these circumstances, it is hardly surprising that growth in commodity-dependent countries has been slow – in the case of many African countries over the past decade, more or less zero. As population has risen, per capita income has fallen, and poverty has grown.[9] Official projections of the distribution of economic gains from the GATT agreement confirm that trade liberalisation will increase, not diminish, global inequality (see Panel 12).

Witness Box 5

Trading Fair
By Christian Aid

It's a small world. Our everyday decisions – about which coffee to drink, which shoes to wear or which bank to use – impact on poor people on the other side of the planet. And, increasingly, the decisions they are forced to make – to chop down trees, to migrate in search of work, to grow drugs – are impacting on us. Some people, those who have the knowledge, organisation and resources to take advantage of the opportunities, are doing very well out of the new global economy. Meanwhile, the gap between richest and poorest widens.

Christian Aid hears the stories of people like Elizabete and her children in Brazil. For most of the year they work from dawn to dusk to pick 84 pounds of coffee. For this they receive £3. And people like Lova Constant in the Dominican Republic, one of thousands of 'congo' workers on sugar plantations, so-called since their ancestors arrived in slave ships from the Congo. She gets paid about £1 for each tonne of sugar cane cut.

Christian Aid has exposed the reality behind the marketing hype in the sports shoe industry. A pair of trainers may sell for £50 or more in Britain, but the 40 or so workers in the Philippines who make the shoe share just £1 of that price between them. It has campaigned on behalf of women growing flowers in Colombia, poisoned by the pesticides that guarantee perfect blooms for our markets.

These stories are too easily lost or hidden in the complexities of global business and trade. In its campaigns for decent wages and safe working conditions, Christian Aid is trying to put fairness back in the picture. In developing countries across the world it supports the efforts of women's, community and church groups to bring pressure for a better deal. It runs joint campaigns, linking Third World and First, shadowing and challenging the networks of production and influence developed by transnational corporations.

Christian Aid believes that citizen action can help influence the terms of trade. As consumers and investors, individuals can bring their ethical values to bear on business choices. Local groups can campaign to persuade supermarkets to stock fairly traded products, or multinational corporations to change their corporate practices. Political action can exert democratic political control over the rules which govern firms, investors and financial institutions.

None of this reduces the responsibility that Southern governments must also bear for the poverty of their own populations. In many countries economic mismanagement, gross corruption, the highly unequal and unreformed structure of landholdings and the general disregard of political elites for their own people have contributed to worsening conditions. International factors have not operated alone.

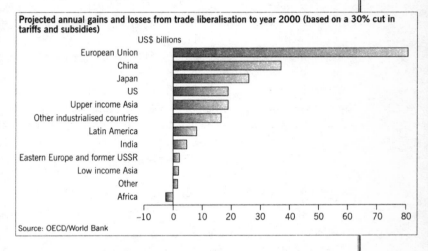
Nevertheless, it remains true that the terms on which many developing countries have entered the new global economy have not been favourable. They have been compounded by debt. Contrary to media perception, the debt stock of the developing world continues to rise, with repayments absorbing over a quarter of export earnings in most indebted countries.[10] Not only are these sums therefore not spent on health, edu-

cation, nutrition and poverty reduction: they frequently exceed those that are. To earn them, many countries have turned to exploiting vulnerable natural resources (such as forests, fisheries and marginal lands), causing severe environmental degradation and further poverty.[11]

There can be no question that debt – combined in many cases with severe economic mismanagement and political corruption – made some kind of economic policy reform necessary in many developing countries. Moreover it is true that in several, particularly in Latin America, such adjustment has helped to reduce inflation and to attract foreign investment. But too often the particular 'structural adjustment' measures imposed by the IMF and World Bank (lessened only partially by recent modifications to Bank policy) have placed the burden of change onto the poorest citizens. Reductions in public expenditure have hit social programmes in education, health, sanitation and family planning. Labour market deregulation has forced down wages, as deflationary fiscal and monetary policies have raised unemployment. Deregulating agricultural markets has primarily benefited large-scale commercial producers, while poorer farmers have been crippled by higher interest rates. In most of Africa, despite these social costs, structural adjustment has not led to macroeconomic stability or growth.[12]

Tellingly – as the World Bank has had to concede – the structural adjustment strategy has not been followed by the most successful of the East Asian economies. In South Korea, Taiwan, Singapore and Malaysia, land reform has kept the distribution of holdings fairly equitable, and care has been taken to maintain credit and infrastructure for small farmers. Public investment in education, health care and urban infrastructure has been made on a very large scale. It is notable that in all of these countries, the distribution of income is much more equal than in any of the countries following characteristic World Bank/IMF prescriptions, and poverty correspondingly less.[13]

The increase in foreign investment flows to the South over the last decade has helped to raise growth rates in some countries. Increasingly, this has encouraged Northern governments to regard such flows as a replacement for aid (indeed, almost a privatisation of it). But foreign investment cannot play this role, for two reasons. First, it is only going to a very small number of countries: about a dozen, in fact, in East Asia and Latin America. The entire continent of sub-Saharan Africa receives less foreign investment than Malaysia alone, just 0.5 per cent of world flows.[14] Reliance on such flows is therefore leaving billions of people without the resources to escape their poverty, non-participants in the new global economy.

But second, direct foreign investment carries its own price. It is attracted by reducing labour costs. This can mean holding down wages to near subsistence levels: for example, in the export processing zones of Mexico and South East Asia. Human rights frequently fall victim, particularly in the intimidation of trade unions. In sub-contracting sectors, working conditions are often dangerous and industrial injuries common. Meanwhile environmental standards are either flouted or not enforced, resulting in endemic pollution and often severe ill health amongst people living near manufacturing plants.[15] In their desire to attract such investment, Southern governments frequently find themselves competing with one another to offer transnational corporations the largest tax breaks and the lightest regulation.

The point of these arguments is not to deny that certain countries in the South, and certain social groups within them, are now experiencing rising living standards. This is to be welcomed. Nor is it to argue that poverty is entirely caused by international economic policy; poor government, corruption and economic mismanagement in many developing countries have also been major factors. The point is that the processes which are generating wealth are at the same time creating poverty. The problem is therefore not 'lack of development', but the path development is taking. Further advance down this path – the path of globalisation on the trade liberalisation/structural adjustment model – will not succeed in eliminating poverty; it will increase it. The gap between rich and poor, both between and within nations, will continue to rise. A new direction is therefore required.

Redefining International Security

The evidence that current patterns of international trade and development are exacerbating poverty should be sufficient reason in itself to seek to alter them. But this is not the only argument. Increasing global inequality is not merely immoral and economically wasteful. It is also dangerous.

Within individual countries, growing poverty leads almost inevitably to social division and conflict. Political instability, authoritarian government and abuses of human rights are then natural corollaries. The last decade has seen much progress made towards democracy and human rights in the South. But as several Southern commentators have noted, these gains cannot and will not survive the prolonged absence of economic and social development.[16] From the Chiapas uprising in Mexico to the civil war in Sudan, from the anarchy now engulfing Sierra Leone to the political and human rights crisis in Nigeria, the mutually reinforcing character of poverty and political instability is evident. The 1994 UN Human Development Report categorised eight of the world's poorest nations as on the verge of catastrophic social disintegration and national breakdown, and named nine others, all in the developing world, requiring international assistance to avoid similar conditions.

An inexorable consequence of poverty-related conflict is the movement of people and the creation of refugees. (See Witness Box 6.) The world is now home to around 48 million people officially designated as refugees,

Panel 13

Refugees

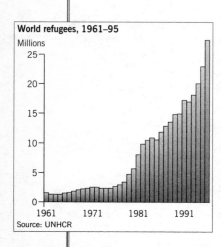

World refugees, 1961–95

Millions

25 —

20 —

15 —

10 —

5 —

0 —

1961   1971   1981   1991

Source: UNHCR

The graph shows the number of 'official' refugees and other 'persons of concern' to the United Nations High Commissioner for Refugees. Official refugees are those who have left their country because they have a well-founded fear of persecution. Other persons of concern include people internally displaced within their own countries, 'returnees' continuing to receive UNHCR assistance, and others in refugee-like circumstances. The UNHCR estimates that there are an additional 21 million internally displaced people worldwide not included in these figures. The rise in the number of official refugees has averaged 12% a year since the mid-1970s.

Source: UNHCR, *The State of the World's Refugees* 1993 and 1995 (Geneva: UNHCR, 1993, 1995).

Poverty and Conflict

By Oxfam

The media-driven public perception of conflict as a brief emergency, to be followed by rehabilitation and the return of normality, is far from the truth. In many of the countries in which Oxfam works, conflict is now a permanent reality to which communities adapt through elaborate survival strategies.

One such conflict is taking place in southern Sudan. It is a conflict which has rarely figured on the UN Security Council agenda, perhaps because it has not attracted the attention of CNN. Yet for the past 12 years, communities in this region have been trapped in the midst of one of the world's most brutal and least reported civil wars, which ranges different groupings in the south against the Government in Khartoum. At least a million people have died, and another 15 million have been driven from their homes either into camps, across borders or into the bush. Behind these statistics are the stories of people like Amer Kuay, a young Dinka woman from the Upper Nile District. This was her testimony to an Oxfam staff member:

'We were attacked by cattle raiders working for the government. They took all of our cattle. They burned our houses. They took all our belongings... We were left with no tools and hardly any seed, so we harvested very little. By February we started to starve. There were still attacks by Nuer raiders. So we decided to cross the Nile to Yirol District where it was safer. Some of the people in our group were dying of hunger even as we started to walk from our village. Young children and old people died. I lost my youngest girl. She was just two years old.'

Both Government and separatist forces in Sudan have shown themselves willing and able to violate the most basic rights of people in pursuit of their military goals. In the lakes Province of Bahr el Ghazal, where Oxfam is involved in supporting relief and rehabilitation work, civilians have been subjected to attack and aerial bombardment. All factions in the conflict have been responsible for burning villages, stealing or destroying crops and livestock, and raping women.

The conflict in Sudan illustrates how tribal and ethnic tensions can underlie strategies designed to disrupt food systems, destroy social life and rob people of their means of survival. These strategies have left some 7.5 million people vulnerable to the effects of conflict and drought – among them people like Amer Kuay.

'internally displaced' within their own countries, or in similar circumstances.[17] Mass migration causes immense social and political pressures. In sub-Saharan Africa fifteen countries contain a million refugees or more, or have a population in which one person in ten is a refugee.[18] (See Panel 13.)

Environmental degradation adds a potent extra ingredient to this mix.

In many parts of the world, notably in the Middle East and in the watersheds of India, Pakistan and Bangladesh, dwindling water supplies are causing political tension and threaten military conflict.[19] In 1994 alone there were 28 conflicts between nations over fishing rights as catches outstripped supply.[20] Meanwhile deforestation, soil erosion and desertification are forcing increasing numbers of people, particularly in Africa, to leave their homelands. Detailed estimates suggest that there are now approximately 25 million 'environmental refugees' in the world. If current trends of degradation continue, it is estimated that this figure could rise to 50 million by 2000, and if global warming has the effects currently projected, to 150m by 2050.[21] This would constitute 1.5 per cent of the world's expected population then, almost a quadrupling of the proportion now.

The industrialised world cannot insulate itself from these concerns. Indeed, it has contributed to them. Its arms sales – 40 per cent of which have gone to 'conflict countries' in the last decade[22] – too often provide the means of war and repression. Its economic policies have frequently made instability worse. The World Bank imposed a severe structural adjustment programme on Rwanda in 1992 even as civil war was breaking out. Refusal to reschedule Algeria's crushing debt burden helped lead to the victory of fundamentalist parties in the 1992 election, subsequently (and with the EU's implicit support) annulled. The ensuing violence, still continuing, has claimed thousands of lives.

The costs of poverty-related conflict and migration inevitably rebound onto richer countries. Coping with conflict has absorbed ever larger sums of international assistance, as witnessed by the huge – and yet still inadequate – expense of humanitarian operations in Somalia and Rwanda. Such costs greatly exceed those which would be required for prevention: in the first four months of its military operation in Somalia, the US spent the equivalent of the entire annual budget of UNICEF.[23] Other kinds of costs too have become apparent. The international drugs trade, for example, starts among poor farmers in Colombia, Peru and Bolivia, for whom the cultivation of narcotic crops provides one of the few viable sources of livelihood in conditions of collapsing commodity prices and debt. (See Witness Box 7.) It makes the connection between poverty in the South and social ills in Britain very stark.

The Drugs Connection

By the Catholic Institute for International Relations

Why do Andean peasants grow crops which, after chemical treatment, end up on our streets as illegal narcotics?

- Because there is a heavy demand for the end product in Britain, Europe and the US.

- Because they get a better price for their crop than other crops that they are at present able to grow, such as coffee.

- Because the drugs cartels buy directly from them, cutting out transport costs.

- Because their families would go hungry if they did not.

The story of narcotics production and the drugs trade is a by-product of the failure of our international agricultural trading system. It feeds on poverty in both North and South.

One important crop is coca. The harmless leaf is central to indigenous Andean culture, chewed as a social and religious ritual and effective in combating altitude sickness and other ailments. The drugs cartels treat it with imported chemicals to turn it into the narcotic cocaine.

CIIR works with Andean peasant organisations in Latin America that want a fair global trading system in order to enjoy basic human rights: to be able to make a living, not to be targets for the drugs cartels, the drugs control agencies, and corrupt military forces. They want demand for drugs in consumer countries to be tackled - not violent military attacks and destruction of their fields with pesticides.

They specifically want coca leaf to be taken off the list of UN narcotic substances so that coca tea can be made for export, providing a legal income, foreign exchange for Andean countries and a healthy herbal drink for the North.

Profits from the international drugs trade are second only to those of the oil trade. They are made mainly by the drugs barons and by the suppliers in the North, and the money laundered throughout the banking systems. CIIR believes that what we trade and how we trade it are ethical issues, and young people in our inner cities and Andean peasants are linked by failed trading structures in urgent need of change.

Perhaps most of all, the mass migration of peoples cannot be confined within the Third World. Officially-defined refugees now constitute just a proportion of the world's migrants: poverty alone is sufficient incentive for people to move. From Cuba to Albania, from Algeria to Mexico, the combination of international inequality and global communications has led inevitably to immigration pressures on the richer nations, as poor peoples seek the better lives they see there. The consequences of population movements on even a fraction of the scale envisaged from further environmental degradation are incalculable.

Concerns about immigration in Europe are already fuelling the growth of racism and violent xenophobia, and thereby adding to the fears of established ethnic minority communities. But the British and European response has been, not to address the issue, but merely to shut it out, attempting to 'ringfence' Southern Europe militarily and tightening already harsh immigration rules. The widespread concern expressed at the British government's proposals to restrict benefits to asylum seekers and to force employers to check the immigration status of job applicants has illustrated how such an approach can lead to fears of increased racial discrimination. But these methods cannot work. As pressures grow, 'fortress Europe' will inevitably require heavier and more expensive policing, with violations of human rights a constant risk. The only viable approach is preventative: to tackle the causes of large-scale migration from developing countries at source. This can only be done, in turn, through long-term development which reduces poverty, maintains the productivity of the environment, and thereby provides security for people in their own lands. Providing support for such development will increasingly be revealed as in the direct interests of the richer countries.

Globalisation and British Economic Policy

There is a final reason why poverty in the Third World must be taken seriously in British politics. The economic processes of globalisation do not simply affect the countries of the South. They are having significant effects on the British economy too.

This is most obvious in those highly publicised cases where transnational corporations have transferred production from Britain (as from other European countries) to locations in East Asia, in search of lower wages. Even when there is no actual transfer of production, a proportion of foreign investment in the South represents lost investment – and therefore foregone employment – in Britain and Europe. One widely-quoted study suggests that competition from Third World imports has reduced the demand for unskilled labour in the industrialised world by 15 per cent in the 1980s alone.[24]

This argument needs to be made carefully. Although there has been some transfer of UK production, it has not as yet been on a very large scale (much less than the relocation between the US and Mexico, for example), and not all foreign investment in the South would otherwise have been made in the North, certainly not in Britain. Only a small proportion of Britain's imports come from the South: most of Britain's trade is with the countries of the European Union and the rest of the industrialised world. Moreover, the growth of consumption in the South, made possible by foreign investment, increases demand for Northern, including British, exports; it therefore adds to employment here. Whether the overall effect of increasing globalisation on employment in the UK has (so far) been positive or negative is consequently a matter of some dispute.[25]

In fact, whichever is the case, there is a second and arguably more important issue at stake here. It concerns not direct job loss, but the way in which globalisation of the economy affects the conduct of British and European economic policy. There are two principal concerns.

The first is that the international regime of free trade, capital mobility and market deregulation acts as a constant pressure on social and environmental standards. Combined with the now rapid processes of technological change, increasing international competition forces companies and governments to seek ways of cutting costs. This is having a direct effect not just on wages but on the conditions and security of employment, as firms look for maximum flexibility and productivity from their employees – in white collar occupations as well as blue collar ones. Moreover global competition acts as a downward pressure on employment protection, social security and consumer protection standards, as arguments over the European Social Chapter have demonstrated. Environmental policies which are seen to raise costs – even if this is only in the short term – similarly become more difficult to defend. Taxation and public spending themselves come to be regarded as costs, raising prices and driving away foreign investment, and are therefore to be reduced.

This in turn leads to the second concern, which is that increasing trade liberalisation threatens the sovereignty of democratic policy making. This is not a question of such sovereignty passing upward from nation states to supranational institutions, but of it being eliminated altogether, as the demands of free trade become paramount. There is particular concern that the constitution and policy of the new World Trade Organisation will militate against national attempts to protect environmental and social standards, regarding these as 'barriers to trade'.[26]

But the loss of government sovereignty extends to economic policy itself. The deregulation of international capital markets – which followed the collapse of fixed exchange rates in the early 1970s – has made the global economy considerably less stable. The huge growth in speculative capital flows makes for large exchange rate fluctuations, in turn forcing governments to adjust interest rates and revise domestic fiscal and monetary policy for reasons unrelated to productive performance in the real economy. The British Government's devaluation and ignominious withdrawal from the European Exchange Rate Mechanism in September 1992 – following speculative attacks on the pound – showed the power international capital markets now have over domestic economic policy (as well as the problems caused by an overvalued exchange rate). France, Portugal, Spain and Italy have all suffered similar experiences in recent years. When the Managing Director of the International Monetary Fund calls for reform of the foreign exchange system because of its disruptive effects, it is clear that something is wrong.[27] Meanwhile the ability of individual traders to cause the collapse or undermining of two international banks in 1995 – Barings and Daiwa – has revealed just how little control national authorities now exercise over the financial markets.

In these ways economic globalisation links Britain and the developing world. The same forces – international competition, trade liberalisation and the movements of capital – affect all economies simultaneously. The same transnational corporations operate throughout the globe. We cannot ignore the processes of poverty creation in the South, because the same processes – at their other end, as it were – are affecting economic policy in this country.

Towards International Security: The Social Regulation of Trade and Capital Flows

We have argued that the current path and structure of international economic development requires reform, in two related aspects. On moral and economic grounds, and to promote international security, concerted efforts must be made to reduce and eventually eliminate poverty. To protect social and environmental standards in both industrialised and developing countries, and to ensure that governments (at whatever level) retain economic sovereignty, the markets of international trade and capital flows need to be better regulated.

From these objectives flow four principal fields of reform. The first is aid. Britain's aid contributions, which have never reached the UN's target of 0.7 per cent of GNP, have been declining over the last fifteen years – the most recent cut being made in the 1995 budget – and now stand at only 0.31 per cent.[28] They should be increased, but they should also be re-oriented. The Pergau dam affair revealed just how far removed from poverty alleviation some of Britain's aid programme has now become. This was sadly confirmed by the British Government's opposition to the so-called '20/20' proposal proposed at the UN Social Summit in Copenhagen in March 1995. The idea that 20 per cent of Northern aid, along with 20 per cent of developing countries' spending, should be directed at basic human development needs is practical, would have an immediate impact on poverty, and should be adopted. Particular priority needs to be given to programmes aimed at raising the status and economic independence of women, providing land and credit for small farmers and enterprises, and enabling the poor to sustain the productivity of their natural environments.

The second, and in terms of impact more important, field of reform is international debt and financial assistance. Again, a compact between Northern and Southern nations could provide a new framework for debt relief, building on the important but far from adequate progress made in recent years. For the severely-indebted low income countries, over 80 per cent of the debt owed to governments should now be written off, in return for commitments to poverty-related development strategies. Multilateral creditors, such as the IMF and the World Bank, must also accept the principle of debt reduction. At the same time the higher priority given in the last few years to poverty reduction by the World Bank should be reflected more clearly in Bank–IMF budget stabilisation programmes, protecting the poorest citizens from the burden of necessary economic adjustment. Institutional reform of these institutions – increasing the representation of developing countries on their decision-making bodies, opening up their procedures to public scrutiny, and establishing proper consultation on projects – would help to reinforce this priority.

Witness Box 8

David and Goliath – Taming the Multinational Giants

By the World Development Movement (WDM)

Today countries around the world welcome global companies and the jobs, technology and investment they bring. Yet behind the promises of prosperity is a hidden danger. Seeking to increase their profits, companies play off one nation against another, forcing them to undercut each other and to bargain away their people's rights.

But increasingly people are speaking out against the global giants. From the Ogoni people of Nigeria outraged by the destruction of their land by Shell, to the toy factory workers in Asia demanding an end to long hours and unsafe working conditions, people around the world are uniting to take on the companies.

The World Development Movement responded to a call from Arunsee Situ, a Thai trade union leader: 'I would like the British people to bear witness to the conditions for workers in other countries.' These conditions led to one of the world's worst ever factory fires in May 1993, when 188 people died in the Kader toy factory in Thailand. They died because the fire exits were blocked and there were no fire alarms or sprinklers. The Kader company, making toys for multinational firms to sell all over the world, had ignored workers' safety to make the toys as cheaply as possible.

These toys are sold in British toy shops for British children. So survivors of the Kader fire and non-governmental organisations in Hong Kong contacted WDM, along with trade unions and campaigning groups in other industrial countries. They documented case after case of unsafe conditions in toy factories and drafted a Safety Code for the companies to adopt. WDM then lobbied toy companies in this country, backed by the prospect of a consumer campaign.

It worked. Only months after the launch of the international campaign, the global toy companies adopted an International Safety Code to improve working conditions for toy workers. There is still much to do to get the Code implemented, but the first move against the modern day Goliaths has been taken.

Third, the philosophy underlying the regulation of international trade needs to be revised. Trade liberalisation on its own is not appropriate. Just as domestically, and within the European Union, markets are publicly regulated to protect social and environmental standards, and support is given to the most disadvantaged regions, so the same principles need to apply at the global scale.

The social regulation of trade requires a number of linked changes. Northern protectionism needs to be reduced. Developing country exports, particularly those with more value-added, need to be allowed greater access to Northern markets. In line with the principle of assisting poorer regions, the World Trade Organisation should provide for preferential trade terms for developing countries in specific sectors on which they are dependent. Agricultural export dumping should be ended, and protection for domestic food production in the South permitted.

The multilateral trading system should also be designed to promote rather than undermine environmental protection and to ensure that the benefits of trade feed through to wages and conditions as well as profits. There is therefore a strong case for membership of the WTO to be linked to respect for minimum internationally-agreed labour standards (based on International Labour Organisation conventions) and comparable minimum environmental standards. Positive steps, such as resource and technology transfer, should be taken to help countries meet these standards. Sanctions, such as import protection, should be available as a last resort, but democratic and accountable enforcement mechanisms must be established first. In addition to their incorporation by the World Trade Organisation, such rules could be enforced by the European Union through a code of practice on the foreign operations of transnational corporations.

A new international trade settlement would have other elements, such as agreements to raise commodity prices over time, and to encourage the transfer of technology, particularly environmental technologies, from North to South. Concerted efforts should be made to reduce the arms trade (see Witness Box 9). Support should be given to trade between Southern nations. The basic philosophy underlying these reforms, however, is what constitutes the crucial change. Freer trade should no longer be thought of as an automatic good. Just as with other markets, trade can have external costs. Just as with other markets, it needs to be regulated to control these costs, and therefore to maximise its benefits.

This philosophy of regulating markets for the general good also underpins the fourth field of reform, in the international financial system. Both areas will require major institutional changes – though the new World Trade Organisation at least provides the structure for this in the trade arena.

Witness Box 9

Ending The Arms Trade

By MEDACT – *Medical Action for Global Security*

Over 400 armed conflicts have occurred since the end of the Second World War. These have caused the deaths of over 20 million people directly and an estimated one and a half billion indirectly. Poor people in poor countries, mostly civilians, have been the greatest victims. The rich countries have supplied most of the weapons.

Even before a bullet is fired, military spending costs lives. It diverts money, scarce resources and skills away from meeting basic human needs. In some countries, more than twice as much money is spent on arms as on schools and health care. Total world military spending stands at around $750 billion a year – equivalent to the annual incomes of the poorest half of the world's people.

Britain is one of the world's largest suppliers of arms. Through the Defence Export Services Organisation – devoted specifically to the task – and through substantial credit guarantees, the Government gives greater support to arms sales than to any other British export. 80% of British arms go to Third World countries. Indeed, as the Pergau dam scandal showed, British development aid has been used as a sweetener to support arms sales to several countries.

Landmines are a particularly appalling kind of export. Mines kill and maim tens of thousands of civilians in areas of past and present conflict. Responding to an international campaign, supported by MEDACT, most European countries now support a worldwide ban not just on the sale, but on the manufacture and use of anti-personnel mines. The UK Government still reserves the right to produce, import, stockpile and use anti-personnel mines.

MEDACT believes that international security will not be achieved through military spending. In particular we believe that a world free of nuclear weapons and biological and chemical weapons is a practical possibility, and can be achieved in stages between now and the year 2020. Many studies have shown that military spending generates fewer jobs per pound than spending on civilian production. MEDACT argues for the establishment of a defence diversification agency to enable the conversion of armaments industries to beneficial, peaceful purposes and to promote retraining and reskilling programmes for their workers.

As progressive disarmament makes a 'peace dividend' available, expenditure should be directed at real security: on social development for the poorest people in the Third World, on environmental protection and on conflict mediation. It is these activities which will promote genuine peace and stability in the post-Cold War world.

Since the breakdown of the Bretton Woods regime 20 years ago, there has been no comparable framework in international finance, and the deregulation of capital flows in the 1980s has only made this worse. It has become increasingly clear that only a new regime of financial stability, backed by an accountable international institution, will permit governments to control economic policy for the common good. In particular, there is a growing realisation – among central banks, as well as independent observers – that speculative flows will have to be controlled: an international tax on currency speculation, for example, is one possibility.[29] It would seem inevitable that the question of national controls on financial flows is reconsidered at the same time.

There can be no illusions about the difficulties of changing the current international economic order. But it seems clear that if reform is not achieved, the problems of global poverty and environmental degradation will get much worse, and will increasingly come to threaten international security. This is not likely to be accepted tamely by Northern societies. Isolationism and protectionism are already major political forces in the US, and racism and xenophobia have increased markedly in Europe. These phenomena represent a response to insecurity which can only fail; by ignoring the causes of the problems they promise simply further conflict and social tension. The alternative approach is the one advocated here: a gradual, agreed, managed shift in international economic relations to tackle the sources, not just the symptoms, of conflict and migration.

Reducing international insecurity in these ways will require increased resources to be directed to the South. But this would not be unprecedented. Following the Second World War the Marshall Plan ensured the stability of Western Europe by financing its reconstruction: between 1948 and 1951 the US gave aid of almost 2 per cent of its GNP, the equivalent of nearly $100 billion a year today. By the end of the Cold War period the West was spending over $500 billion a year to safeguard its security against the perceived Soviet threat. For the Gulf War, at a time of recession, a further $54 billion was collectively found.[30]

The threats we face today are not primarily military. They are less visible, more diffuse. But they are just as serious – for the world's poor and their environments, they are already a matter of life and death. They force us to reassess what we mean by 'international security', and how in today's world it can best be protected. If just a small proportion of the annual resources devoted to military defence during the Cold War or the Gulf crisis were redirected into the new, post-Cold War threats of environmental degradation, population growth, migration, social breakdown and armed conflict, the trends to international instability and insecurity could be reversed.

Some figures can be put on this. The United Nations Development Programme (UNDP) estimates that an additional $30 billion in development aid over the next ten years would be sufficient to meet the basic nutritional, health, sanitation and education needs of the 1.3 billion people living in absolute poverty, with a further $10 billion required to make family planning services available to all.[31] This is the equivalent of 5 per cent of global military expenditure, or 6.25 per cent of industrialised countries' military spending. Ending absolute poverty, in other words, would cost about 3 weeks' worth of arms, or one-fifth of the rich nations' existing annual 'peace dividend'.[32] In practice, it has to be recognised that more than this is going to be required, to support long-term development, reduce environmental degradation, contain conflict and limit migration. The UNDP proposes the establishment of a 'global human security fund'. Set at, say, $150 billion pa over the next five years, this could largely be financed through the imposition of an international currency speculation tax of 0.05 per cent. $150 billion is a large sum, 0.6 per cent of global GDP. But military spending during the Cold War represented more than 4 per cent of global GDP.[33] Whatever figures we choose, the problem is not money. It is political will. As the costs of continued inaction are increasingly recognised, current policy will surely appear more expensive than reform.

A Children's Agenda
By Save the Children

Each generation should leave to the children of the next generation a world at least as diverse and productive as the one it inherited.

In both North and South, powerful forces of change are disrupting human societies and increasing human insecurity. Poverty is a key component of this, undermining the lives of individuals and communities and threatening destitution or, at its most extreme, life itself. People in poverty are excluded from participation in their societies and are unable to exercise their rights as citizens or retain their proper dignity as human beings.

Children bear the heaviest burden of poverty. Throughout the world, whether in the more affluent or in the poorer countries, children are much more at risk of living in poverty than the population as a whole. A new commitment to social development is needed. But for SCF this must involve fundamental changes in the way adults (and particularly those in positions of authority) value children and their rights. Why?

Because childhood is a once-and-for-all window of opportunity for biological and social development. Children are vulnerable and need extra support. Failure to support development in childhood has permanent and irreversible effects for individuals, denying them the opportunity to reach their full potential.

Because children are the most powerless group of all – they have no electoral or coercive power. They are the group with the least capacity to influence their own treatment.

Because failure to support development in childhood has a massive impact on society's capacity to develop in the future, as the lost potential starves the economy of the human capital needed to ensure future growth-with-equity.

Neglecting children means neglecting a social group which already plays an important role in social and economic development, and whose inclusion in social development benefits all. Children are important social actors now, in the present, as well as being the adult generation of the future. Children's experience of their treatment by adult society will mould their own approach to social development, encouraging exclusion and discrimination, fear of others and division.

Save the Children believes that the way societies regard and relate to children is a litmus test of their commitment to human or social development as a whole. Within the constraints and opportunities of its context, culture and resources, every society must therefore be judged according to its commitment to a Children's Agenda.

Inequality and the Quality of Life:
Repairing British Society

For Richer, For Poorer

If increasing inequality has been the experience of the world as a whole over the last 20 years, the same is true within Britain. The report of the Rowntree Foundation's *Inquiry into Income and Wealth*, published in February 1995, showed how the UK's economic growth over the past 30 years has been distributed.[1] In the period 1961–79, the incomes of the poorest 20 per cent of the population grew at or above the average rate for society as a whole, while those of the top 20 per cent rose slightly more slowly than the average. From 1979 to 1992, average incomes in Britain rose by 36 per cent, with those of the richest 20 per cent growing faster than this (the top 10 per cent by over 60 per cent). But the incomes of the poorest 20 per cent of the population failed to rise at all, and those of the bottom 10 per cent actually *fell* by 17 per cent.

As a consequence, the gap between rich and poor has grown larger (see Panel 14). Indeed, according to the OECD, the UK now rivals the US as the most unequal of all the industrialised societies.[2] Since 1977, the proportion of the population with less than half the average income has more than trebled. 3.7 million children – one in five – now live in families dependent on Income Support (the social minimum or 'safety net'), or on less than this. Income inequality is particularly stark in terms of ethnic origin, with more than a third of the ethnic minority population in the poorest fifth of the population as a whole, compared with only 18 per cent of white people. Poverty disproportionately affects women: two-thirds of the adults in the poorest households are women, and nearly 60 per cent of lone parents (90 per cent of whom are women) live on less than half average income.[3]

Inequality in Incomes

Income inequality in the UK, 1962–90

Index of inequality (Gini coefficient)

Source: JRF

The upper graph shows trends in income inequality in the UK since the early 1960s. The higher the index, the more unequally income is distributed. Between 1962 and 1977 incomes became gradually (if somewhat unevenly) more equal. Between 1979 and 1990 there was a rapid rise in inequality, by 10% between those dates. The level of inequality reached was almost back to the 1938 level estimated by the Royal Commission on the Distribution of Income and Wealth.

The graphs below show the income changes underlying the increase in inequality. The left

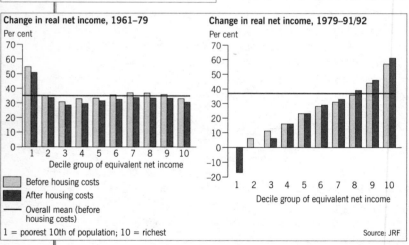

Change in real net income, 1961–79

Per cent

Decile group of equivalent net income

Before housing costs

After housing costs

Overall mean (before housing costs)

1 = poorest 10th of population; 10 = richest

Change in real net income, 1979–91/92

Per cent

Decile group of equivalent net income

Source: JRF

hand part shows the growth in net real income between 1961 and 1979 for successive tenths of the population. It shows income both before deducting housing costs and after deducting them. The right hand part shows what happened between 1979 and 1991/2. Since 1979 the lowest income groups have not benefited from economic growth, in contrast to the earlier period.

Source: Joseph Rowntree Foundation, *Inquiry into Income and Wealth* (York, JRF, 1995)

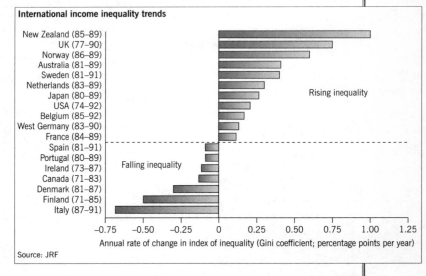

Panel 15

International Comparison of Income Inequality

The graph shows the annual rate of change of inequality in different countries over recent years. Only in New Zealand has income inequality risen as fast as in the UK. Inequality has been rising in many industrialised countries, but in most of them this has been at less than half the UK rate. In several inequality has been falling.

International income inequality trends

New Zealand (85–89)
UK (77–90)
Norway (86–89)
Australia (81–89)
Sweden (81–91)
Netherlands (83–89)
Japan (80–89)
USA (74–92)
Belgium (85–92)
West Germany (83–90)
France (84–89)
Spain (81–91)
Portugal (80–89)
Ireland (73–87)
Canada (71–83)
Denmark (81–87)
Finland (71–85)
Italy (87–91)

Rising inequality

Falling inequality

−0.75   −0.50   −0.25   0   0.25   0.50   0.75   1.00   1.25

Annual rate of change in index of inequality (Gini coefficient; percentage points per year)

Source: JRF

Source: Joseph Rowntree Foundation, *Inquiry into Income and Wealth* (York: JRF, 1995).

In human terms, increasing poverty is manifested in many different ways: in the numbers of people living on the streets and in desperately inadequate accommodation (see Panel 16), in the inability of more than 6 million Britons to heat their homes to a reasonable level of warmth,[4] in the falling life expectancies and much worse health of the poor in comparison with those on average incomes (see Witness Box 11), in the creation of particular neighbourhoods and housing estates where poverty, poor education, crime and drug abuse are concentrated.[5] In its various aspects, poverty makes life bitterly hard, sometimes desperate, for millions of Britain's citizens. (See Witness Box 12.)

Homelessness and Housing Need

The graph shows the number of households accepted as homeless in Great Britain (England, Scotland and Wales). Local authorities are only obliged to accept people in 'priority need' (those pregnant, with children or otherwise vulnerable) who are not categorised as having made themselves 'intentionally homeless'. Many single people, particularly young people, are not included in the statistics. Most of those sleeping rough are not included. In 1994 only a third of those who presented themselves to local authorities were accepted as homeless under the legislation. At the end of 1994 there were 52,377 families living in temporary accommodation (including bed and breakfast and hostels) in England, Wales and Scotland.

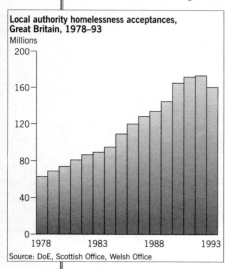

Local authority homelessness acceptances, Great Britain, 1978–93

Millions

Source: DoE, Scottish Office, Welsh Office

In addition to the statutorily homeless, and the 'hidden homeless' (those staying in other people's homes, in overcrowded conditions, etc), many households face the threat of homelessness because of mortgage arrears. At the end of June 1995 there were 209,600 mortgage-holders six months or more in arrears, and in the year to that date 49,390 repossession orders were made against home owners in England and Wales, or nearly 1000 a week per annum. Many other people live in inadequate housing. The English Housing Conditions Survey conducted in 1991 estimated that there were almost 1.5 million dwellings which were unfit for human habitation. A report published by the Joseph Rowntree Foundation in 1995 calculates that to meet housing need in England alone, 117,000 affordable permanent homes are required each year for the next twenty years.

Source: Department of the Environment, Scottish Office and Welsh Office, collated (to 1993) in J Newton, *All in One Place: The British Housing Story 1973–93* (London: Catholic Housing Aid Society, 1994); Council of Mortgage Lenders, *Arrears and Possessions Statistics*, (July 1995); Department of the Environment, *The English Housing Conditions Survey* 1991 (London: HMSO, 1993); A Holmans, *Housing Demand and Need in England 1991 to 2011* (York: Joseph Rowntree Foundation, 1995)

Poverty has a number of causes, but predominant amongst them is unemployment. As is well known, total unemployment has risen drastically in the last 20 years: from 425,000 people in 1973, or 1.7 per cent of the labour force, to 2.24 million, or 8 per cent, in November 1995. Long term

Unequal Health

By the Public Health Alliance

Health means more than just being free from illness and disease. It means access to fulfilling employment, having the resources to keep ourselves fit, secure and independent. And it means an environment free from pollution, hazards and risk. Despite all the social and medical progress we have made in this century, we are still faced with many avoidable hazards to health and are challenged by enduring health inequalities.

The movement which is often referred to as 'the new public health' takes into account the environmental, economic, and social influences on health. One of its most important principles is that of equity, which requires the removal of avoidable and unfair differences in access to good health.

This demands a reduction in poverty. Poverty affects health in a number of ways:

- It restricts the means to secure good housing, food, warmth and the ability to participate in society.
- It can cause stress and anxiety.
- It limits people's choice and ability to bring about health-promoting changes in behaviour.

The link between income and health has been well documented since Sir Douglas Black's report on Inequalities and Health in 1980. More recent research shows some stark inequalities between the richest and poorest people. Out of the 66 main causes of death for men, 62 are more common in the poorest social classes (IV and V). In women 64 out of 70 are more common in these social classes. In recent years increased poverty and unemployment have been responsible for the return of tuberculosis as an important disease in Britain.

The latest research (by Richard Wilkinson) goes further and suggests that it is inequality itself that causes ill health. Increasing life expectancy now depends less on economic growth than on reducing income inequalities. International comparisons of countries with similar levels of national income show that where income is more evenly distributed throughout society, not only does poorer people's health benefit, but also the health of the whole society.

Health is a fundamental good. Its promotion should be the aim of government policy. But this requires changes not just to health policy, but to the very idea of economic development itself.

unemployment (more than a year) has risen from a few thousand in 1973 to 825,700.[6] (See Panel 17.) This is the officially unemployed. A further 1,238,000 people are not even attempting to seek employment any more.

Witness Box 12

Poverty in the UK
By Church Action on Poverty

Society is dividing before our eyes. The gap between rich and poor has grown remorselessly over the last 20 years. Global economic changes coupled with specific public policy choices made by successive governments since 1979 have led to the UK becoming one of the most unequal industrialised countries in the world.

Whilst the causes of poverty are often complex its impact is deeply personal. It is felt by those individuals, families and communities who find themselves increasingly excluded from the benefits of a wealthy society. Poorer people have poorer health, reduced opportunities and lower life expectancy. In some areas more than half the adults are out of work and the majority of families are struggling to survive on means-tested benefits.

The voices of those directly affected by poverty are powerful and need to be heard, as some of the statements made by people at CAP's local poverty hearings demonstrate.

'Poverty makes us sick.'

'To be poor is to be labelled.'

'Poverty puts so much pressure on families that all but the strongest break down.'

'Long term poverty is the deadly enemy of hope.'

Central to Christian belief is the fact that we are all one body, one creation. Social and economic division, therefore, is an affront to God as well as to our human dignity.

It is imperative that we act to remove poverty and reduce inequality. Whilst this will require radical changes in economic and social policy the solutions cannot simply be imposed from above. The restoration of hope, confidence and community requires the direct involvement of those who have lost so much in the 1980s and 90s. Social justice must be built from the bottom up as well as from the top down.

These are the prematurely retired, those taken off the unemployment register onto incapacity (invalidity) benefit, women for whom a job wouldn't pay because of the structure of the benefit system, and so on.[7] Poverty is exacerbated by the redistribution of employment between households. Work is increasingly concentrated: 60 per cent of households are 'work-rich', having two earners, while 19 per cent are 'work-poor', with no earners at all. Individuals living in workless households not only have lower incomes: they are increasingly unlikely to get back into employment at all. Most new jobs go to individuals from households with an adult already in work.[8]

Panel 17

Unemployment

The graph shows the number of people officially registered as unemployed – that is, claiming benefit and actively seeking work – and the number of vacancies notified to job centres. The criteria for eligibility for unemployment benefit have changed a number of times over the past fifteen years. This has left large numbers of people uncounted by the official claimant-based statistics. Most of these are included in the data gathered by the Labour Force Survey (LFS). The 'Standard' LFS definition of unemployment corresponds to the International Labour Organisation measure, counting as unemployed those who have not undertaken any paid work in the previous week, who want work, are available to start within 2 weeks and who have looked for work in the previous 4 weeks. This measure added 244,700 people to the unemployed figure in August 1995, making the total unemployed 2.56 million. Given the low level of vacancies, the 4-week job search criterion almost certainly underestimates the number of people wanting employment. The LFS 'Broad' definition relaxes this criterion. Under this measure a further 983,500 people were unemployed in August 1995, taking the total to 3.54 million.

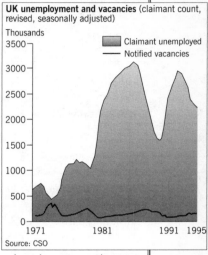

UK unemployment and vacancies (claimant count, revised, seasonally adjusted)

Source: CSO

Source: Central Statistical Office NOMIS on-line database, December 1995; Labour Force Survey, Central Statistical Office, calculated in Unemployment Unit, *Working Brief* No 71, February 1996.

The other principal factors contributing to the growth of poverty are changes to the rates and system of welfare benefits, including the ending of the link between benefits and pensions and earnings; and changes to tax rates and the increase in indirect taxation. The largest single factor is the reduction in relative wage rates at the lower end of the scale, including lower incomes among the increasing numbers of self-employed.[9]

Of course, rising inequality is not universally regarded as a bad thing. The predominant economic defence of inequality is that it is necessary to increase national wealth. The rewards for success and penalties for failure act as the spur to improved economic performance. Inequality encourages growth, and growth will then generate higher incomes for everyone, including those at the bottom.

But there is little evidence to support this view. The British economy did not grow faster in the 1980s, when inequalities grew, than in the previous decade when they declined. Most of Britain's most successful competitors – Germany, France, Japan, Italy – have more equal distributions of income than Britain.[10] On the contrary, inequality is costly: it requires higher public spending on social security, it increases the economy's propensity to import (since higher income households consume more imports than poorer ones) and it increases the volatility of economic cycles.[11]

The real defence of inequality is therefore in fact to be found elsewhere. It is less often stated, but it has been implicit in the politics of recent years. It is that poverty for some is the regrettable price of making the majority better off. Since so much of the increase in inequality has taken the form of a direct redistribution from the poor to the more affluent – in the combination of benefit and tax changes, for example – it is hard to escape the conclusion that this argument is at work. And indeed politically it appears to have succeeded. Whatever the injustice involved in such a utilitarian calculus, it is true that the incomes of the majority have risen sharply over the last two decades, and this state of affairs has apparently won electoral support.

The Costs of Inequality

But there is a price to be paid, and it is becoming increasingly clear what it is. For inequality is not only damaging to the poor themselves. By destroying social cohesion, it affects the standard of living of everyone in society.

The decline in social cohesion takes a number of forms. It is manifested in the segregation of experience among people of different income levels. Certain neighbourhoods become ghettos of high unemployment and poverty. Long-term unemployment and the increasing use of means-tested benefits separates into two distinct groups those paying for state welfare and those dependent on it. Middle class parents opt out of local community schools. Declining public transport comes to serve only the poor. When contact between social groups collapses, so people trust and

Food Poverty
By The Poverty Alliance

In Castlemilk, a deprived housing estate in Glasgow, it is easier to find a pre-prepared Black Forest gateau than it is to find a fresh cauliflower. Why?

Some of the poorest people have the greatest difficulty in accessing an adequate supply of affordable, quality food. Lack of money is part of the problem: there are no agreed budgetary standards to determine, for instance, the food element in welfare benefits. But so is the operation of the global food market. As the market connects the cheapest points of production with the most profitable points of sale, the needs of poorer, disempowered consumers are increasingly overlooked. As a consequence low income households, especially those who live on the periphery of towns and cities, are reduced to a limited choice of high priced goods. With the lion's share of the UK food market in the hands of a few supermarket chains, the independent suppliers who serve the poor compete on added value rather than on nutritional standards or value for money. So you can get cooked packaged meals in Castlemilk and estates like it, but good quality fresh fruit and vegetables are hard to find. Poor people not only end up paying more, their health and that of their children suffers.

Community organisations have attempted to address food poverty in a number of ways: most commonly by setting up food co-ops and by raising peoples' awareness of the benefits of healthy eating. But the impact of these measures has been limited. Many activists are exhausted by the effort of using their voluntary labour to protect their communities from increasing food prices. What is required is a radical change in the system of food production and distribution. People's need for nourishing, healthy food should be put first. Communities must be empowered to give them greater control of their food supply.

Building on the existing work of our members in combating food poverty, the Poverty Alliance is conducting an extensive, participative enquiry into alternative systems for meeting communities' food needs.

care about one another less and there follows a widely felt loss of the sense of 'community'. It is no surprise then that those marginalised by mainstream society feel disaffected by it – whether manifested in the apathy of low voting turnouts or more dramatically (as seen again in 1995 in Luton, Leeds, Bradford and Brixton) in the angry frustration of urban riots. But perhaps the most potent symptom of the decline of social cohesion is the growth of crime.

It seems certain that much crime is related to social exclusion: to the alienation felt by people who through unemployment and poverty are

Panel 18

Crime

The graph represents the number of crimes (excluding criminal damage of less than £20) recorded by the police in England and Wales. (Equivalent figures for Scotland are not directly comparable.) The figures are given per thousand of the population in order to adjust for changes in the population over time. Recorded crime has risen from about 1 per 100 people in the 1950s to 10 per 100 in 1994.

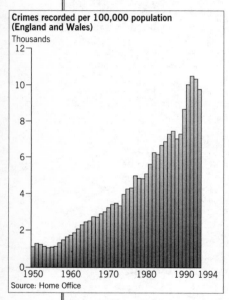

Crimes recorded per 100,000 population (England and Wales)

Thousands

Source: Home Office

Since not all crime is reported to the police, the British Crime Survey (BCS) asks people about their experience of crime. The BCS estimates the total number of crimes committed in 1993 as 18 million, nearly four times the number recorded by the police. Of crimes recorded by the BCS, 20% were violent crime (wounding, robbery and common assaults) and 19% were incidents of vandalism. 10% were burglaries, 24% thefts of vehicles (including attempted thefts); and 27% other kinds of theft. Sexual offences are omitted from the published figures because trend data are unreliable. (The recorded crime figures show sexual crimes increasing in recent years. Part of this may be due to increased reporting.)

The British Crime Survey show that rates of crime are higher in inner city areas than outside. However the *increase* in crime has been greater outside inner cities than within them. People living in council and rented accommodation and in flats are most at risk of crime. Afro-Caribbean and Asian people experience more crime than white people.

Whether or not they have actually experienced it themselves, many people are fearful of crimes being carried out against them. In the 1995 British Social Attitudes survey, a quarter of men and a third of women reported that 'worries about crime affect their everyday life', for example where they go or what they do.

Sources: Home Office, *Information on the Criminal Justice System in England and Wales*, Digest No 3, 1995; Home Office Research and Statistics Department, *Research Findings*, No 14, 1994; L Dowds and D Arendt, 'Fear of Crime' in R Jowell et al (eds), *British Social Attitudes: The 12th Report* (Aldershot: Dartmouth Publishing, 1995).

unable to participate in the consumption and opportunities of the society around them.[12] In neighbourhoods and among social groups where unemployment reaches 50 per cent and more, where most young people have never had a job and have little prospect of getting one, it is unsurprising that many people feel little stake in society or concern for others. Crime, drug abuse, vandalism and anti-social behaviour frequently follow – particularly amongst young men, who seem to be offered so few sources of masculine identity where jobs are scarce, and for whom violence as an outlet for frustration must often seem legitimised by popular culture. The sanctions of previously cohesive communities are now absent.

The principal victims of crime are the poor themselves; but crime powerfully connects the wellbeing of the middle classes to the poverty around them. As crime rates rise year on year, fear of crime has become one of the most salient features of our collective experience. It affects not only our basic feelings of personal security, but our relations with strangers, the sense of trust which lubricates so much of ordinary social life. Most women know this only too well. (See Panel 18.)

The consequences spread throughout society. Few children walk to school nowadays as they did 20 years ago; so car-ferrying parents have less time and more stress and traffic congestion rises.[13] In general parents become more anxious about their children's safety, and limit their opportunities to play.[14] Crime has sent insurance premiums soaring. It contributes to the decline of town centres, as shoppers feel safer in out-of-town shopping centres.[15] More money is spent on security equipment and services of all kinds, both by households and by businesses, raising costs and reducing real incomes. Public expenditure on policing, prisons and the judicial system grows inexorably: virtually doubling in real terms in the last 20 years.[16]

For evidence of what happens when inequality and social exclusion grow beyond a certain point one has only to look at conditions in many American cities. The creation of an apparently permanent underclass, unattached to the rest of society, has made crime, violence and drug abuse endemic. Their reach has spread well outside the inner cities themselves to affect the quality of life of every urban citizen. Britain does not yet face social breakdown on this scale, but the trends are evident.

The Quality of Life

The argument here parallels that concerning poverty in the Third World. It is unjust that the poorest groups in society are getting poorer, when society as a whole, and especially its richest citizens, are becoming wealthier. It is particularly immoral that poverty should be caused, in part, by a deliberate redistribution from poor to rich. But it is also counter-productive. For increasing inequality does not ultimately make even its apparent beneficiaries better off. As social cohesion breaks down, the costs of increasing inequality rebound on everyone.

The political significance of these trends in fact goes beyond this, for they call into question the whole basis of the dominant model of economic and political activity. This is the assumption that having more income necessarily raises people's standard of living. An alternative view suggests itself: that if in generating wealth society creates social costs which then damage individual wellbeing, there may come a point where people feel their quality of life is no longer rising. They may feel they would actually be better off with less money income, but correspondingly fewer social costs.

Crime is by no means the only cost which is prompting people to thoughts of this kind. Environmental degradation is another. Environmental problems increasingly impact directly on individuals and families. 1.3 million children in Britain – that is, one in seven – suffer from asthma, now shown to be aggravated, and possibly caused, by traffic pollution.[17] This is causing daily anxiety in literally millions of households. Traffic congestion also increases stress, reduces the conviviality of neighbourhoods and adds hours in every week to journey-to-work times. The loss of countryside and natural habitats – from roads, quarries, landfill sites, housing and many other kinds of development – affects increasing numbers of people: not just local residents and recreational visitors, but a wider public whose sense of nature and culture feels increasingly violated. The rise of environmental protest, from roads to animal welfare, is surely testimony to this. Fear for the future – for the effects of environmental problems on the lives of present children – adds a powerful extra dimension.

As with crime, of course, environmental problems do not simply

Housing and the Quality of Life

By the Town and Country Planning Association

Our housing system is in crisis.

- An estimated half-million people are homeless.
- The backlog of needed housing repairs now runs to £20 billion.
- After the price-inflation of the 1980s the private housing market is now static; many families are trapped in homes which are inappropriate either in size or location, and many have 'negative equity'.
- Over the last 50 years, cities have been emptying, as those who can afford to escape a steadily worsening urban quality of life do so.
- There is immense pressure on the countryside from house-building, exacerbated by the inability of the market to redevelop many derelict sites in urban areas.

The latest projections suggest that there will be an extra 4.4m households – an increase of 30 per cent – by 2014. Most of this growth comes from the structure and dynamics of demographic change, as people leave home earlier, divorce more readily and live longer. However much urban redevelopment takes place, this demand will place more pressure on the countryside.

In recent years, the nation's responses to these trends have been:

- Protecting mortgage tax relief because of the subsidy it gives to 'Middle England', while preventing local authorities from spending their capital receipts on building new homes.
- Ritual conflict over the release of land for housebuilding, between volume housebuilders taking their opportunities on 'greenfield' sites and local residents seeking to protect their amenity, many of them recent incomers themselves.

One hundred years ago, the TCPA's founder asked 'the people: where will they go?'. The same question applies today. It might be possible to protect the environment (and the amenity of the 'haves') by cramming people into existing urban areas and restricting land supply and public finance in order to suppress demand. But this will not be acceptable if it merely forces the 'have-nots' to live in over-crowded conditions or to travel impossible distances to jobs and amenities. New solutions are demanded.

Environmental protection, affordable housing for all and quality of life are possible. But they require of politicians nationally and locally a leap of imagination and courage in order to bring equity and quality back to our planning and housing system.

reduce wellbeing directly. They also have financial costs: in medical care for illnesses related to pollution and fuel poverty, in insurance premiums for environmental damage, in the costs of transport delays due to congestion, and so on.

A third area of social cost has come to increasing attention in the last few years. This is insecurity and stress at work. For some time a feature of manual occupations, insecurity is also becoming pervasive among white-collar and professional workers. (According to recent figures, between 1992 and 1994 a third of all employees experienced at least one period of unemployment.[18]) This is in part a consequence of technological change, now occurring rapidly in the service sector. But to a considerable extent it has also become a deliberate management strategy for organising work, as businesses displace risk onto their employees. The pressure of competition gets transmitted into personnel strategies designed to achieve maximum 'flexibility': short-term contracts, part-time and variable-hours work, performance-related pay, and so on. The recent well-publicised case at a nationwide hamburger chain, where employees were given 'zero hours' contracts requiring them to clock off when there were no customers waiting to be served, was by no means an isolated one.[19] The long-term effect on productivity is contradictory at best – insecurity damages morale and undermines investment in training – but the effect on the quality of individuals' working lives is plain. Insecurity increases stress and reduces wellbeing.[20]

Long hours of work have the same effect. Over the last ten years, despite a drop in the total number of full-time employees, the number working 45 hours per week or more has increased significantly – from 4.7 million in 1984 to 5.7 million in 1994.[21] For many employees this extra work is unpaid: longer hours represent an enforced increase in personal productivity, which inevitably take their toll on mental health and wellbeing. Longer hours and stress in turn cause a variety of family and social problems as less time is spent with partners and children.[22]

From all these areas – crime, environmental degradation and insecurity and stress at work – a pattern emerges. National income is rising. Personal incomes, for some, are rising. But people do not feel that they are getting better off. We have evidence of this from opinion surveys and it is confirmed by various measures of welfare which go beyond mere income.[23] And indeed, despite the challenge to conventional wisdom which it represents, it is now a commonplace in national political debate. Here the gap between income growth and wellbeing is known quaintly as the 'feelgood' factor, and its absence widely noted. But it remains a source of puzzlement. Politicians and commentators who have long taken it for granted that the expectation of rising income is what makes people happier wonder vainly why it is not doing so at the moment.

At least part of the explanation surely lies in the increasing significance of social costs. Personal disposable income is not all that people need to make them 'feel good'. Wellbeing also consists in the enjoyment of a range of social goods – personal security and the absence of fear of crime; clean air; pleasure in nature and other aspects of environmental quality; confidence in the future; security and enjoyment at work. When these social goods are absent or declining, many people may feel that their overall quality of life is falling – even if, at the same time, their personal disposable income is rising.

Indeed, it is not just social goods of these sorts. More conventional public goods are also components of the quality of life: the condition of the national health service and the expectation of its care; the quality of children's schooling and the standards of the education system in general; the flourishing of the arts and popular culture; even the state of democracy and the condition of national institutions. All these too constitute aspects of individual feelings of wellbeing. The decline of many of these public goods in recent years has left many people with a tangible sense of national decay. When so many people feel so anxious about the world their children will inherit – indeed, about their children's lives even today[24] – it is hardly surprising that they do not feel good.

In this way the conventional notion of 'the standard of living' – personal post-tax income – is seriously misleading. The 'feelgood' factor represents the missing element between personal income and the wider concept of wellbeing, or quality of life. It is raising overall quality of life which should be the goal of economic and political activity, not simply individual incomes. And this in turn is not just about the wellbeing of individuals, but about the health and flourishing of society as a whole.

The political implications are quite profound. First, all these social and public goods require social action and public expenditure. Personal incomes cannot secure them; however much income the average citizen earns or is 'given back' in tax cuts, he or she cannot use it to escape the effects of crime, or social breakdown, or air pollution, or ozone depletion,

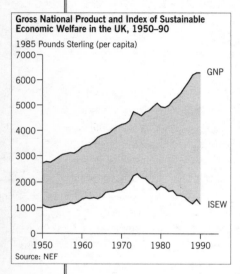
or the insecurity of employment conditions. Private spending cannot reduce the sense of national decay that arises from inequality or the decline of public goods. These are social costs and they can only be reduced – that is, social goods can only be provided – through public expenditures and regulation. Contrary to the insistence of the dominant economic and political view, public spending may make individuals and households feel better off than personal spending does.

Second, and consequently, the divergence between personal income and quality of life casts doubt on the primary goal of conventional politics.

Redefining Wealth and Progress
By the New Economics Foundation

For all our sophistication, modern society still persists in making one huge leap of faith. We blithely assume that if at the end of the day, one key indicator of economic output – GNP – goes up, the quality of life of the citizenry will improve.

At both neighbourhood and national level, there is increasing evidence that this is not so. Freedom from crime, security in work, environmental quality and a convivial community all make contributions to welfare that go unmeasured in conventional economic tallies.

Though politicians typically lag behind, these arguments are now widely accepted. They are leading to the development of new, alternative indicators of economic progress.

One 'headline' indicator has been launched in the UK by the New Economics Foundation: the Index of Sustainable Economic Welfare (ISEW). Tracing ISEW between 1950 and 1990, the UK appears to be barely better off than it was in the mid-1970s. The reason is clear: a rising toll of social and environmental costs that are increasingly reflected as real losses in terms of welfare. The 'externalities' not accounted for by mainstream economics are coming home to roost.

At a local level, the New Economics Foundation has helped local government to develop community-based sustainable development indicators, measuring directly the things that really contribute to local quality of life. 10 per cent of the UK population now has such indicators available locally.

NEF has also worked with ethical businesses such as Traidcraft, Happy Computers and Body Shop to develop the 'social audit'. This is a way of assessing the impact of an organisation on people's lives. It offers a unique tool to help improve the positive impact – the 'social performance' – of any business or organisation.

New indicators such as these go to the heart of democratic debate, by looking at how we measure the success of politicians, economists and society. If we continue to ask the wrong questions, we will continue to get the wrong answers.

83

Raising the rate of economic growth, given its current patterns, will not improve people's wellbeing. These patterns are generating the social costs – inequality, crime, environmental degradation, insecurity, the decline of public services and public goods – which are reducing people's perceived quality of life at the moment. More of the same will only exacerbate these costs. And there is no guarantee that rising personal income will compensate for them. The feelgood factor will then continue to elude conventional politics.

In terms of economic policy there is an obvious conclusion to be drawn. If the ultimate goal of policy is to raise personal and social well-being, its principal objectives should not be to maximise the rate of economic growth and growth in personal disposable income. Rather, attention should be paid to the various factors which contribute to quality of life, and these should be pursued directly. These include incomes, but they also include a variety of social goods, including a lessening of inequality, reduction in crime and environmental improvement. A crucial dimension in doing this will be to change the indicators by which progress is measured. Mainstream political debate remains in thrall to Gross National Product as the primary index of national welfare, despite its well-established inability to capture most of the important aspects of quality of life.[25] There is an urgent need now to replace it in this role with more meaningful measures. An indicator such as the Index of Sustainable Economic Welfare, for example, makes strong claims (see Panel 19). Indeed, the mere occurrence of a public debate about alternative indicators would begin to change the political context in which economic and social policy was discussed. Such a debate is long overdue. (See Witness Box 15.)

Taxation, Welfare and Public Goods

The two trends highlighted here – rising inequality and falling quality of life – come together in the intertwined issues of taxation, public spending and the future of the welfare state. There are few fields of politics in which public debate has failed so abjectly. At budget time now, it seems, we must witness the unedifying spectacle of our two principal political parties competing to cut income tax, urged on by newspapers delighting in the cynical claim that a 2p or 3p cut is all that is required to buy the votes of the British public, while every other issue pales into political insignificance besides.

The crude simplicity of this argument debases the morality of public debate. When income tax cuts which disproportionately benefit those on higher earnings are paid for in part by reducing the funds going to young people on housing benefit, disabled people in long-stay hospitals, and health and clean water projects for the poorest people in the Third World – and this rates barely a mention by most of the media – the ethics of the contemporary political process are grimly revealed.[26]

But the ramifications of the restricted debate about tax go further than this. The underlying assumption – quite explicit, and yet entirely unquestioned – is that only one side of the budget equation really counts. The politicians and pundits pronounce on whether changes to tax rates have left us 'better' or 'worse' off. What taxation pays for seems not to enter the frame. Yet the evidence from so many areas of British society suggests that public spending, or the lack of it, makes an enormous difference to individual quality of life and to the wellbeing of the nation. If taxes (whether direct or indirect) are reduced, and this demands lower expenditure on education, or health care, or crime prevention, or public transport, is it really obvious that we are better off? And if not, why is public debate conducted as if it were?

The effect is felt most perniciously in the field of welfare reform. If poverty is to be tackled, the first task is to increase – and redistribute – work, as we shall argue below. But there can also be little question now that the functioning of the welfare state must be reviewed.

The details of a reform package are not the most important issue here. Some elements are obvious: starting tax rates and household benefit conditions must be integrated so that those on welfare can enter the labour market without losing all their benefits and thereby suffering penal rates of effective marginal taxation (the so-called 'poverty trap'). Other possible reforms should be given wider public airing and debate, such as the proposal that compulsory saving schemes should be established to pay for national insurance and pensions, with the funds administered by non-governmental bodies.[27] The notion of an unconditional citizens' income to replace means-tested benefits and tax allowances has also attracted interest.[28]

But all of these proposals share a common theme. This is that the incomes of the better off must be taxed at a level sufficient to remove from poverty those who cannot otherwise earn enough. Such a redistributive principle lies at the heart of the concept of social justice, and if poverty is to be eliminated it cannot be shirked. It has three different implications.

First, the progressivity of the tax system must be restored, including not just income tax and VAT but inheritance, capital gains and corporation taxes. Many of the tax changes made in recent years have been regressive in effect, giving more to the better off – in some cases, very much more – and penalising the poorest.[29] British businesses pay less tax than in any other leading industrialised country (yet investment is still among the lowest and the net flow is out of the country, not inward).[30] Equity demands that the richest sections of society contribute the most.

Second, the debate about the future of the welfare state must not get stuck in the assumption, now commonly made, that the only direction in which welfare spending can go is downwards. Despite its sharp rise in recent years, it is simply not true that welfare spending has become unaffordable. At 14.6 per cent of GDP, the UK's social security budget is proportionately among the lowest in the OECD.[31] This is largely because of the poverty in which welfare recipients in the UK are kept; it is thus intimately connected to the faster growth in inequality in Britain reported earlier. But in turn this means that such poverty can be reduced through welfare spending, particularly if employment levels can be raised as well. Britain's public finances are not in crisis: at 36 per cent of GDP, the government's current receipts are well below the European average of 45 per cent.[32] In terms of borrowing, the OECD projects that by 2000 the UK's public debt will have fallen to just 47 per cent of GDP, the lowest in Europe; the European average will be 70 per cent.[33] There is room for more welfare spending because there is room for higher taxation.

It is this, thirdly, which is the central issue. In recent years, with some honourable exceptions, British political debate seems to have frozen around the idea that tax rises are unconscionable. Increases have occurred, notably in VAT. But they have been regarded with universal horror: as self-evidently distasteful and to be reversed as soon as possible. The particular facts of these cases are not the issue here, but the principle is crucial. When tax rises become politically taboo, we begin to lose our capacity for self-government. Taxes pay for public goods, and these can provide benefits to society and to individuals which private spending cannot. The under-provision of such goods in the UK today is glaring, from education to the health service, childcare to public transport infrastructure. If taxes must rise to pay for them – particularly income taxes – then this is the membership fee we pay for living in a civilised society.

The elimination of poverty is a public good of this kind. Its principal

Witness Box 16

People Matter
By the Employment Policy Institute

People are the world's greatest resource. Yet human affairs are often conducted and spoken about as though people don't matter. Indeed throughout the world mass unemployment is used as a means of economic management.

Such an outcome is neither desirable nor inevitable. While the causes of unemployment are complex, the chief culprit is bad economic and social policy. In the UK, unemployment costs £23 billion per annum and causes untold misery and suffering. Alongside serious ill health, to become unemployed is the fate we all fear.

On top of this nearly a third of the workforce are in insecure jobs. 50 per cent of households are a paycheque away from disaster, having £450 or less in savings. Workers in the UK have to work longer for less pay than their counterparts in the rest of Europe.

Technology and trade offer opportunities to achieve far higher levels of employment through the management of supply and demand. The Government should invest in job subsidies to encourage employers to take on long-term unemployed people. It should create a tax and benefits regime which encourages, rather than penalises, work at the lower-paid end of the labour market. And it should itself invest in the public sector, thus creating jobs and meeting needs. The EPI believes that people do matter and that the Government should make a commitment to the goal of full employment as a basic priority of economic and social policy.

beneficiaries will be the poor themselves; but as inequality and exclusion are reduced and social cohesion rebuilt, the gains will be experienced by society as a whole.

A New Approach to Work and Unemployment

Restructuring the welfare and taxation systems is important, but if it is to be effective in eliminating poverty it must be matched by a new approach to employment and unemployment. Over the last decade unemployment has been treated in British politics with complacency and a singular lack of imagination: less policy progress has probably been made in this field than on any other major political issue. We must deal with both sides of the coin – not just with the absence of work, but with work itself.

Unemployment is the principal cause of poverty. It also contributes directly to despair and unhappiness.[34] The vast majority of unemployed people lose self-esteem and status, their range of social contacts declines, they lose the structure to the day provided by work, and they feel excluded from majority society – both from the opportunity to contribute to it and from its benefits. Unemployment breeds social alienation, particularly among young people who have never had work, with anti-social consequences. It costs taxpayers approximately £23 billion in benefits and lost taxes – and more to pay for its health and social effects.[35] It is one of the main causes of the rise in welfare spending. Reducing unemployment must therefore become, as it once was, a central national economic priority. (See Witness Box 16.)

Unfortunately, political debate about unemployment is mired in the arguments of the past. The problem lies in the conception both of what 'more employment' means, and how (and indeed whether) it can be achieved.

The notion of 'full employment' still conjures up images of full-time, lifetime jobs for men. This is unhelpful in three different ways. First, women now make up almost half the workforce, and the proportion is still rising. Providing employment for all who want it is therefore a considerably larger task than it was when something close to full employment last obtained in 1973. Second, a quarter of workers work less than 'full-time' hours.[36] Part-time employment is often derided as 'not proper work', but this is a predominantly male attitude. Some part-time work is involuntary, but much of it is not. Surveys show that many women want to work part-time, particularly when their children are young (and household income is sufficient). Many people who currently work long 'full-time' hours would like to work fewer if they were able to. (Some part-timers would like to work more hours, though not necessarily full-time.)[37] Given the variety of patterns of working hours now experienced, the distinction between 'full-time' and 'part-time' work has ceased to serve a purpose. Both in law and practice therefore all employees should receive equal treatment irrespective of working hours. The goal of employment policy, meanwhile, should be to provide the *hours of work*, at fair rates of pay, that everyone wants.

The reason that many women desire less than 'full-time' work is because they want to do other things with their time, particularly to spend it with their children. This is because, third, paid employment is not the only form of work or activity which is important, either to society or to individuals. Looking after children, caring for elderly and disabled dependants, education and voluntary work are all equally valid and worthwhile activities. This isn't just true for women – or it shouldn't be. Society would benefit enormously if men spent more time with their children, and so would men and children – not to say women. The economy, as well as many individuals themselves, would benefit from time taken out for further education. The community at large – its cohesion, its care for the most vulnerable, its cultural and social diversity – would gain enormously from greater voluntary activity.

Society's goal should therefore not be simply to increase *employment*. It should be to enable people – both men and women – to do the variety of kinds of *work* which provide benefit to themselves and to society; in different combinations at different periods in their lifetime. Caring and voluntary work, in particular, need to be officially recognised and properly valued, with benefits available accordingly. Particular priority should be given to caring for children: not only through enlarged professional childcare services (though these are strongly needed) but by enabling parents – fathers as well as mothers – to work shorter hours and to take time away from employment.[38] The quality of the time given to parenting is crucial to the education and socialisation of children: increasing that time, and reducing the stress experienced by working parents, should be central goals of employment and social policy, with benefits to wider society as well as to family life. Lack of childcare is also what keeps many lone parents – and therefore their children – in poverty, since it makes them ineligible for employment.[39]

Increasing the variety of working patterns in this way will require changes in national insurance structures, benefits and pensions, and more flexible methods of redistributing earnings over lifetimes, both by employees and employers. The growing adoption of early and part-time retirement, along with employers' schemes for 'career breaks', sabbaticals and maternity and paternity leave, already point in the required direction.

The longer-term goal should be to reduce 'normal' full-time working hours. This would not only be good for employees; as experience in the German engineering industry has shown, shorter hours can make a significant contribution to creating employment.[40] The key to 'redistributing work' in this way is the willingness of employees to trade money for time, for example by taking (part of) a wage rise in shorter working hours. Tax incentives, for both employers and employees, could be provided to encourage this. While many people cannot afford to reduce their earnings, particularly when interest rates and mortgage payments are high, it is absurd that many people work long and stressful hours – more of them than they want – while others have no work at all. Incentives for voluntary work redistribution therefore make much sense.

Of course, none of the foregoing is to say that providing more jobs – including more or less 'full-time' jobs for currently unemployed men – is not still important; it is vitally so. The current debate on how this can be done, however, is remarkably unconvincing.

From one end of the political spectrum comes the call to make labour markets more 'flexible', reducing wages (and benefits) and making it easier for employers to hire and fire workers. The high rate of job creation in the US is cited to show the efficacy of this approach. But this does not stand up to scrutiny. Once the size of the US economy, population growth and under-recording of unemployment are taken into account, job creation in the US has not been significantly better than in the 'inflexible' labour markets of European countries. Downward pressure on wages is maintained substantially through the willingness of immigrants to work for very low pay. (A permissive immigration policy has not noticeably been one of the policies of those who favour labour market deregulation in Britain.) Moreover the price of 'flexibility' has been large. Real wages in the US have fallen for two decades, leading in the last five years to a substantial decline in average family incomes. Low wages have dramatically increased poverty. Since a reduction in poverty is a primary reason for wanting higher employment (or at least is said to result from it), this strategy simply defeats itself.[41]

Lower wages are not an effective means of generating higher employment, as detailed studies of the economic effects of minimum wage legislation show.[42] By raising employee turnover rates and discouraging commitment or investment in training, low wages tend to reduce productivity. In the British context they are also extremely expensive. Since employees on low wages can claim benefits to supplement their income, their employers are effectively subsidised. As the wages of the bottom 10 per cent of the labour force have fallen over the last two decades,[43] so the cost of Family Credit has soared, now standing at £1.68 billion.[44] Low wages constitute one of the most important causes of poverty in Britain; the imperative must be to raise not reduce them.

The prescription from the opposite political wing is an alternative approach to the 'supply side'. This is to improve education and training and to encourage investment, to make British industry more competitive internationally. This is indeed a necessary part of any strategy to increase employment, but it hardly seems a sufficient one. Without an increase in domestic demand (or indeed, policies to generate demand internationally), supply side measures alone are unlikely to reduce unemployment very substantially, let alone quickly. Higher investment will only occur if there is the expectation of future demand.

But an old fashioned Keynesian demand expansion (now generally proposed on a coordinated European basis) is also problematic. Over the short term there is no doubt that a generalised expansion would create jobs, particularly if wage growth can be constrained. But the magnitude of the problem suggests humility about the likelihood of 'full employment' being reached by this route. Between the beginning of 1993 and the end of 1995 the British economy grew at an average rate of around 3 per cent per annum, in a manner - in contrast to the 1986-90 period - widely regarded as 'balanced'. Unemployment fell by over 700,000 from its 1993 peak.[45] But even the official level remained two and a quarter million. At this rate it would take a further seven years of growth at an annual rate of 3 per cent to reduce unemployment to below 500,000. Even in the 'golden years' of the post-war boom Britain never achieved such a growth rate for such a period of time. In the present, even envisaging improvements in the economy's productive capacity, the build-up of inflationary pressures and Britain's traditional balance of payments constraint make the prospect of achieving full employment through this means look fanciful. Given current slow improvements in environmental efficiency, the environmental implications of fast, general growth rates must also be regarded as unacceptable.

The problem here is that, if growth takes a conventional, generalised form, a rate of around 2.5 per cent per annum is required before any employment is generated at all. This is because technological change, which raises productivity, allows higher output to be produced with less labour. This effect can be overcome if output rises fast enough, but this will only occur when growth rates are high. Thus occurs the phenomenon of 'jobless growth' – output rising, but too slowly to reduce unemployment.

This process is evidently occurring in parts of the manufacturing sector, but it is often argued that it need not occur in the economy as a whole, since the extra resources generated by growth translate into demand in other sectors. How far this creates employment, however, depends on which sectors experience the additional demand. Much of the service sector, long considered the main 'absorber' of resources generated by manufacturing, is now itself automating rapidly, with widespread shedding of jobs. Demand for consumer goods may rise, but in an increasingly open economy this will not necessarily create more jobs in Britain. Only the personal services, leisure and public sectors, which remain domestic and labour intensive, offer real opportunity for job growth – if spending is directed towards them.

But this begins to take us into a different strategy for raising employment. The goal, it seems clear, must be to increase the 'labour intensity' of growth: that is, the ability of the economy to generate employment even at low growth rates. This leads to two principal objectives: to raise demand in the economy in those sectors where the impact in terms of number of jobs created is highest, and in occupations in which the unemployed (whose skill levels tend to be low) can be employed; and to reduce the costs of employment to employers without reducing wages. A number of policy approaches seem to be available.

The first is a job subsidy for the long-term unemployed. Long-term unemployment is not merely soul-destroying for those who experience it; as far as most employers are concerned people who have been out of work for over a year are effectively no longer in the running for jobs at all.[46] This means that not only do the long-term unemployed not contribute to the economy in terms of production, their unemployment does not even help to moderate wage levels (and thereby assist the general process of employment creation without inflation). Meanwhile the state pays them to be inactive. In these circumstances giving employers a six-month subsidy to take on those who have been unemployed for more than a year would have two effects. For the six months of the subsidy it would give the new employees invaluable work experience, bringing them back into the active labour force. After the six months it would (therefore) increase the pool of employable labour. (In some cases the employee would no doubt be retained by the firm.) In turn this would help to lower the 'equilibrium' rate of unemployment in the economy (the rate at which higher employment generates increasing inflation). This would make it easier to maintain an increase in demand, and therefore higher employment.[47] If the subsidy were set at the average level of welfare benefit already received by long-term unemployed people, the scheme would be virtually costless.

The second policy approach is what has come to be known as 'eco-tax reform'.[48] It is based on the recognition that the current structure of taxation is curiously perverse in the incentives it provides. By adding 10 per cent to employers' wage costs in National Insurance contributions it penalises employment, while by taxing environmental damage hardly at all it gives relative encouragement to resource-use and pollution. Shifting the burden of taxation away from labour and onto energy, transport and waste could therefore make a significant contribution, not just to sustainability, but to employment. Reform of this kind was proposed in the 1993 European White Paper, *Growth, Competitiveness, Employment*.[49]

A number of eco-tax reform studies have now been conducted in mainland Europe and in the UK (see Panel 20). They suggest significant increases in employment could be obtained from a 'fiscally-neutral' reform package (that is, one in which total tax revenues remained unchanged), particularly if employment tax reductions are targeted at the lower end of the wages scale. The employment gain comes about because labour-intensive firms respond to lower wages by employing significantly more people, while energy and resource-intensive ones respond to higher costs with much smaller job losses. In only a few industries – for whom tax rises could be phased in – do these higher costs reduce competitiveness significantly. One scenario modelled for the British economy projects a net gain of approximately 300,000 jobs.[50] Reducing employers' National Insurance contributions, of course, cuts wage costs without cutting wages, and therefore without increasing poverty. Such a policy could therefore bridge the gap between alternative views on low and minimum wages policy.

Panel 20

Eco-tax Reform

'Eco-tax reform' is the name given to a shift in the burden of taxation away from economic 'goods', such as labour and value-added, towards environmental 'bads', such as energy, transport, waste and pollution. Terry Barker of the Department of Applied Economics at Cambridge University has simulated several alternative reform packages for the British economy. These include:

Package 1: A gradually increasing carbon/energy tax is introduced in 1996, with the rate rising to $10 per barrel by 2000. The extra revenue is exactly compensated by reductions in employers' National Insurance contributions. The tax is accompanied by a £1.1bn domestic energy-saving programme to protect the poor. The projected economic results are compared with a 'reference' scenario in which no reform package is introduced and the economy continues unchanged. By 2005 the results are:

- GDP growth is 0.1% more than in the reference scenario.
- 278,000 extra jobs are created and unemployment falls by 200,000.
- Inflation is slightly higher (0.2% pa) than in the reference scenario, and the balance of payments (as a proportion of GDP in 2005) slightly lower (0.2%).

Package 2: Road fuel tax is increased by 5% a year (as is current Government policy), with the revenues recycled by reductions in employers' National Insurance contributions. By 2005 the results are:

- GDP growth is 0.1% more than in the reference scenario.
- 191,000 extra jobs are created and unemployment falls by 100,000.
- Inflation and the balance of payments are unchanged from the reference scenario.

Neither package has a significant effect on international competitiveness; the higher cost of energy is offset by the lower cost of labour.

The European Union recently commissioned a major modelling study of eco-tax reform for the six largest European economies. The policy package includes additional taxes on energy, traffic congestion charges and charges on water effluents, along with various other environmental incentive measures and expenditures on research and development. Revenue from the new environmental taxes is used to finance a reduction in social security payments by employers. The environmental results are significant. In 2010 carbon dioxide emissions are projected to stabilise at 1990 levels, air pollutants to fall by 70–80%, water pollution by 50% and solid waste by 40%.

The economic projections are as follows. By 2010 GDP in the six countries as a whole is 0.06% higher than in the unchanged reference scenario. In the UK it is 0.88% less. Employment is 0.15% higher, translating into a gain of 2,187,000 jobs in the six countries as a whole, and 400,000 jobs in the UK.

Sources: T Barker 'Taxing Pollution Instead of Employment: Greenhouse Gas Abatement Through Fiscal Policy in the UK', *Energy and Environment*, Vol 6, No 1, 1995, pp 1–28; DRI et al, *Potential Benefits of Integration of Environmental and Economic Policies*, (London: Graham and Trottman/CEC, 1994).

We do not underestimate the transitional difficulties that would result from eco-tax reform. Any policy approach would therefore have to be gradual and very carefully formulated. But such difficulties are true of any radical policy designed to address a major social problem, and there is no larger problem than unemployment. Tax packages of this kind have now been introduced in Sweden and Denmark and are under serious consideration in Germany and several other countries. They deserve detailed debate in the UK.

Eco-tax reform would encourage additional employment primarily in the private, labour-intensive service sectors. The third possible approach to raising employment would focus on the public and voluntary sectors. Here we have other lessons to learn from.

A common feature characterises all the European countries which successfully maintained low rates of unemployment in the 1980s – particularly Norway, Sweden and Finland. All adopted some form of 'social contract' in which incomes – not just wages, but executive salaries and dividends – were restrained in return for employment protection. Even more importantly, all maintained large public and public-financed sectors, utilising in relatively high taxation and public spending the resources generated by extremely competitive manufacturing sectors. (In Japan, the other country which did not experience mass unemployment, the same function continues to be served by the personal services sector, which employs more people than the equivalent sectors in European countries. The price for low unemployment is therefore paid in higher prices.)[51]

The same approach seems almost certainly to be required in Britain if mass unemployment, with all its attendant social consequences, is to be ended. Public and voluntary sector employment will have to rise, financed primarily by higher taxation. Given the existing cost of unemployment to the exchequer – which of all examples of 'governments wasting public money' must count amongst the largest – this would not be as expensive as it sounds. But there can be no escaping the requirement to raise taxes, to some degree, to pay for it.

There is of course no shortage of work to be done by a publicly financed employment programme – in the care of children, the elderly and the sick, in building homes, in cleaning up and enhancing the natural and built environments, in installing energy and water conservation measures (which would in part pay for themselves), in recycling, in arts and cultural activities, and so on. There is moreover no reason for this work to be carried out by the public sector itself. Public sector finance can pay for work carried out by both private firms and voluntary sector organisations. Indeed, as we discuss below, the priority should be to use an increase in public spending as a way of strengthening Britain's emerging 'third sector' of community-based and voluntary enterprises.

The strategy proposed here would of course involve an increase in demand, and therefore economic growth. But this would not be generalised growth, as the dominant models of economic policy propose. The goal of policy would be to target spending at sectors which could specifically create employment and meet social needs – and improve environmental efficiency as well. The crucial point is that the effects of economic growth on employment depend on the *content* of growth at least as much as, and probably more than, on its rate. It is quite likely in fact that other ways of expanding demand – for example, by increasing consumer credit – would generate faster growth. But they would create fewer jobs. The priority is not growth *per se*, but employment and the meeting of social needs. It is therefore to these ends that policy should be directed.

Strengthening the Third Sector

Proposals to create jobs through public spending carry the connotation of huge new government bureaucracies on the one hand and cheap, temporary training schemes on the other. We are not interested in either. Our proposal is that a considerable proportion of publicly-raised funds should be directed into local, voluntary and community-based enterprises and organisations, with the twin goals of raising long-term employment and meeting social needs.

Around the country, in many of Britain's most deprived urban neighbourhoods, in its rural areas, and even in its more affluent suburbs, tens of thousands of voluntary, community-based organisations enable local people to improve the conditions of their localities and take some control over their own lives. As Panel 21 indicates, they come in a variety of forms and meet many different kinds of needs, identified by local people. They are already creating jobs, work and incomes. But their activities are barely

Panel 21

The Social Economy or Third Sector

The 'social economy' is made up of firms and other trading enterprises whose primary aim is to meet a social need, rather than to make a profit for private owners. It includes worker cooperatives and other employee-owned businesses, and consumer cooperatives whose ownership is vested in customers. But most enterprises in the social economy – those sometimes referred to as the 'Third Sector' – are owned and controlled by voluntary associations of people who wish to meet particular social needs. All profit made by such enterprises goes back into the business or into the community; none is distributed to private individuals.

Housing associations and cooperatives constitute one of the largest groups of third sector enterprises: though highly professional and in some cases very large, they are run by voluntary management boards whose commitment is to the provision of social housing. Housing associations are often able to lever private investment into a local area, for wider economic development as well as for housing. On local authority housing estates a number of tenant management schemes have turned into tenant cooperatives where ownership as well as control is vested in the residents. Other voluntary organisations provide other social and care services of many different kinds.

The last twenty years has seen a considerable growth in the number of community enterprises, particularly in disadvantaged urban areas but also in some remote rural ones such as the Highlands and Islands of Scotland. These are community-owned businesses whose aim is to create employment for local people, usually by providing locally-needed services. Examples include local shops, neighbourhood security schemes, housing repairs businesses and childcare services. In a number of areas community development trusts have been established to help develop such businesses, usually as partnerships between the local community, the local authority and the private sector.

Credit unions are locally managed associations which make money available at low interest rates to people who would otherwise be forced to borrow from loan sharks (see Witness Box 18). One of the most interesting developments in recent years has been the development of LETS (Local Exchange Trading Schemes), which create an effective 'local currency' to facilitate barter exchange between local people. Other social economy enterprises include food co-ops, where healthy food is bought in bulk at a discount and redistributed locally; recycling and re-use projects for paper, furniture, clothes and other items; environmental clean-up projects; and various kinds of community care services. Youth clubs, play schemes, parent teacher associations, arts and cultural activities and sports clubs are also widespread throughout the country.

recognised by mainstream political debate. Most of them suffer from a severe lack of resources. Given greater support, there is enormous scope for their expansion.

> ## Witness Box 17
>
> ### Community Development in the Inner City
> By the British Association for Settlements and Social Action Centres
>
> People in inner city communities suffer from a number of linked problems:
>
> - Persistent unemployment, especially long-term unemployment.
> - Industrial change and its effect on the labour market, particularly on poorly skilled people.
> - Changes in social and family structures and their increasing breakdown.
> - Social exclusion, especially experienced by women, ethnic and other minorities and people with disabilities.
> - The persistence and spread of traditional forms of poverty which are often concentrated in urban areas and which get worse because of the widening gap between rich and poor.
>
> These factors are leading to growing resentment on the part of those who are excluded from sharing in the nation's wealth or who lack any sense of control over their own conditions. Many are driven to desperate or disruptive behaviour, such as violence or drug-taking.
>
> We need to break out of the cycle in which our inner cities are places where 'if you get on you get out.' BASSAC's experience of over 1000 pieces of work in urban areas teaches us that this can be done where the following factors apply:
>
> - An integrated policy for an area (environmental, economic and social) which is given time to have an impact. Three year projects are inadequate – the timescale needs to be ten or even twenty years of long-term, modest work.
> - Local people and community groups must be admitted as equal players and given support to build their capacity to engage in regeneration partnerships and to manage local assets.
> - Policies must be based on need and sustainability and not on presentation. Competition for resources is no way to conduct a policy for urban renewal.

In both political theory and economic policy, public debate has for too long assumed that there are just two sectors in society, state and private. In fact there are three, and the third sector – both community-based enterprises, and the wider network of larger, often better-funded voluntary organisations and groups – represents a crucial component of a healthy society and economy.[52] It employs around 400,000 full-time equivalent workers (approaching 2 per cent of the total workforce) and contributes £12.3 billion to the gross national product. It is estimated that 4 million people engage in some kind of voluntary work at least once a month.[53]

New Money
By Birmingham Settlement

The old expression 'the poor pay more!' applies especially to credit. Most households require credit to help budget for expensive times, such as Christmas or the start of the school year, and to cope with repairs and emergencies. For low income households this can mean a downward spiral in the stranglehold of debt.

Birmingham Settlement carried out a survey for the BBC *Panorama* programme. We found that low income households on social security pay interest rates ranging from 65 per cent a year for a small secured loan with a pawnbroker to 500 per cent for a similar loan unsecured with a moneylender. The average cost of credit for the poor in Britain is in the region of 250 per cent, or 12 times the charge for credit from a bank for a household in work.

But there are alternatives. A decade ago Birmingham Settlement helped initiate a campaign with the Birmingham Credit Union Development Agency to establish credit unions in the city. A credit union is a 'save and borrow' co-operative. Members save together regularly and borrow as needs arise from the common fund at the maximum charge of 12.63 per cent set by law. At the beginning of the campaign, sceptics predicted that poor people wouldn't save and would certainly default on borrowing. Today this cynical view has been completely disproven with a national average default rate in credit unions of below two per cent. There are now 30 credit unions in Birmingham alone and over 500 in the country as a whole.

Recent years have seen a widespread closure of banks and building society branches in inner city areas. So Birmingham Settlement has initiated the formation of the Aston Reinvestment Trust – the first community reinvestment fund in Britain to provide access to affordable credit in disinvested areas. Aston Reinvestment Trust will initially act as an investment broker for loans to small businesses and start-up enterprises in the Aston area. Later it will move on to develop ethical investment for housing associations and energy efficiency projects in the inner city.

Third sector organisations provide services and activities which neither state nor private sector can. They demonstrate by example ideals of social justice, democratic participation and environmental care – in real life, through practical achievement, not just in theory. They show in new methods of social and environmental accounting how organisations can be governed by ethical as well as financial goals, responsible to all their 'stakeholders', not just shareholders – lessons now being learned by the corporate sector.[54] They manifest and celebrate the diversity of a multicultural nation. And they translate into action the personal motivations of voluntary service and social benefit without which community life is barren. As the applications to the National Lottery funds have shown, it is in the voluntary and community sector that British society finds its most characteristic idealism and vitality.

Economically, community-based enterprises play a crucial role. By keeping income circulating within their own areas, they strengthen local economies, creating jobs from local spending. In many of Britain's most deprived areas, where 'inward investment' is not forthcoming, this is the only possible source of income growth. But in many other areas too, strengthening local economies can help to safeguard employment, reducing dependence on a small number of large employers. For nearly two decades many local authorities have tried to support the development of small enterprises (both private and community) for this reason. But they have been hampered by lack of funds and powers, and by the short-term, frequently-changing nature of central government schemes. What is needed is a long-term commitment to the principle and funding of local economic development. (See Witness Box 17.)

There is particular interest now in the creation of local and regional banks to support local enterprises. (See Witness Box 18.) By international standards the UK's banking system is remarkably centralised. In disadvantaged areas money saved tends to flow out into the international economy with little reinvested or returned. In some areas the banks have withdrawn altogether. By providing finance where the conventional banking system will not, with a specific focus and commitment to their area of operation, local and regional banks have had remarkable success in a number of countries.[55]

Strengthening voluntary neighbourhood organisations will not simply increase employment. It will help to meet social needs directly, providing facilities and services otherwise lacking, particularly in disadvantaged areas. This is by far the most effective form of preventative social policy, creating supportive networks for individuals and families, such as single mothers and young people, trying to cope with stress and poverty.[56] Community-based organisations tangibly raise levels of hope and self-confidence and a sense of social participation. By enabling people to work together for one another, they give expression to feelings of altruism and mutuality, and thereby help to regenerate a sense of community.

The Regeneration of Community

The term 'community' is often used nowadays, and it is often criticised as meaningless. But we use it with a very clear meaning. To speak of 'community' is to recognise that there *is* such a thing as society, and that its health and cohesion affect the wellbeing of everyone. It is to acknowledge that people are not just individuals, pursuing their own independent ends, their only relations with others those of market transactions. We are dependent in almost every aspect of our lives on the neighbours and strangers who make up the rest of society – on their cooperation in a shared moral, legal and social order. Our quality of life depends on social goods which are shared with and can only be provided in association with others. To seek the 'regeneration of community' is therefore to assert that relationships of mutual cooperation between the members of society must be specifically nurtured.

Loss of a sense of community is widely felt in Britain today. Many of its causes lie in deep-rooted and irreversible social trends, such as the breakdown of tradition and changing lifestyles. But it has been exacerbated by the extended reach of market forces in society. In global markets the pursuit of efficiency overrides the ties of geography and culture, pulling workers and their families across countries to new job locations. At one end of this process settled communities are undermined as industries decline and move away; at the other new ones fail to develop, on new housing estates with few public spaces and critically weakened social bonds. These trends are powerful enough in their own right, but in the dominant model of economic development they have been reinforced by ideological celebration. The logic of the market is the pursuit of self-interest. This is morally justified, it is claimed, by the freedom of individual choice markets provide and the wealth they create overall.

But such a logic is self-defeating. For it is precisely where markets have triumphed that self-interest cannot play this moral role. Where the constraints of long-standing cultures and mutual relationships have been uprooted, where people no longer know one another personally, the pursuit of self-interest becomes simply selfishness, a lack of concern or care for others. If this is manifest most starkly in the growth of crime and casually perpetrated violence, it is reflected too in a more general lack of connection between strangers. Is it not this that has bred the reaction 'it's not my responsibility' in those cases where witnesses to crime and violence have failed to intervene? Why parents are ever more fearful of letting their children play unwatched? In the market, we are told, we must look out for ourselves. But in the real world we want our neighbours to look out for us as well. Once market forces have pulled communities apart, self-interest is incapable of acting as moral glue. Neither individual freedom of choice nor general wealth can compensate.

To counteract these trends requires a reinforcement of mutuality and moral care: this is why strengthening community organisations and activities is so important. Yet the example set by government seems to be precisely the reverse. Allowing poverty and homelessness to rise and mentally distressed people to wander the streets uncared for – a cruel irony that this should be called 'care in the community' – can surely only reinforce the general trend towards lack of concern for others. When society seems to say officially that we are no longer responsible for one another, we should not be surprised if people act as if it is true.

In this sense 'community' is centrally related to social justice. Moreover it is not just about local communities. We are a community as a nation, and as such we have the responsibility of a wealthy society to provide at least minimum levels of material welfare to every citizen. This is not just the expression of a healthy community, but a prerequisite for one. Where there is deep inequality there can be no community, for inequality breeds social division. It is social justice which makes for social inclusion, and inclusion which encourages mutual respect and socially cooperative behaviour.

It is because the regeneration of community must be founded on social inclusion that it does not mean – as some have supposed – the imposition of a unitary, dominant culture. On the contrary, in a multiracial and multicultural society this could only be a route to further disintegration. The experience of many of Britain's black and ethnic minority citizens today is one of injustice and exclusion, the result of continuing racial discrimination and (in many parts of the country) increasing racial harrassment and violence.[57] Tackling racism is therefore an urgent priority – not just in its specific form of employment and housing discrimination, but in the more general and pernicious social processes through which

Witness Box 19

Racism, Equality and the Environment
By the Black Environment Network

A colleague came into work the other day and said 'I've just been spat on. Because I am not white. In the streets where I was born, on my home ground.'

Day to day incidents such as these attack our sense of belonging in our own country. When an Asian shopkeeper was attacked in Wales recently and died for not being white, shock waves went through the minority ethnic communities. We feel anxious and unsafe. Our sense of the ownership of our local environment, of the control we have over our lives, is consistently undermined. Yet this is the basis for political participation in society.

Some elderly members of our communities have worked for 30 or 40 years on factory floors and grown old in the inner cities without ever having seen the countryside, for whose care they have paid taxes all their working lives. Many ethnic minority communities live in the most polluted urban areas of Britain, with children who have never experienced what it is like to walk in a wood.

The future of the earth and its people cannot be won in isolation. The majority population of the world finds its continuity within the ethnic communities of Britain. It is only through working towards the acceptance and celebration of Britain as a multicultural society that we may build our way towards an increasingly positive relationship with all the members of the world population. Anti-racism is thus an essential component of sustainable development, at home and abroad. There will never be environmental quality without human equality.

certain ethnic groups face systematically worse educational, income and employment outcomes.[58] It is exclusion in these forms which undermines the sense of community and creates divisions in society, not the expression of cultural and religious difference. As we enter the 21st century the development of a new public consensus about the nature of Britain as a multi-ethnic and culturally diverse society is long overdue. Only on the basis of such a consensus can a sense of national or local community be built. (See Witness Box 19.)

The relationship between social injustice and community in fact works in both directions. The regeneration of a sense of community is in itself required to reduce inequality. We argued above that a form of enlightened self-interest was sufficient reason for even the affluent to desire the reduction of poverty and the provision of other social goods. But enlightened self-interest still requires a leap of faith, from a concern only with one's own private consumption to a willingness to contribute to shared social goods. It is the sense of community which supports this leap; which makes people feel that their own wellbeing is bound up with the wellbeing of others. Social cohesion, for example, is a striking feature of those countries which did not allow mass unemployment to develop in the 1980s: it is the sense of national community which enables higher taxes or prices to be levied. This seems likely to be true in Britain too. Public support for social goods will surely depend on the prior acknowledgement that we live in a shared community and must make decisions accordingly.

The Renewal of Democracy

6

The Democratic Deficit

Public disaffection with the process of politics in Britain is now widely recognised. Social surveys show how little trust the British people have in their politicians and how deep their alienation is from the political institutions which govern them. (See Panel 22.) Politicians and commentators acknowledge the fact. But this has occasioned almost no public reflection on why, or on what could be done about it; still less has it led to any kind of concerned response. The complacency with which the guardians of national democracy treat its decline is perhaps itself the strongest evidence of the need for reform.

This is not about 'sleaze' or standards in public life, as such debate as there is would have us believe. The issues dealt with by the Nolan Committee are merely symptoms of a deeper malady: a political system and a political culture no longer appropriate to the world they govern. For a long time the archaic structures of the British constitution and its political institutions could be dismissed either as harmless manifestations of tradition or as subtle means of administering power. Government, after all, worked – or so it seemed. But economic decline and political malaise give this argument less and less conviction. Increasingly, the processes of good government are seen to be damaged and hindered: by the secrecy and departmentalism of Whitehall; by the inward-looking clubbiness of Westminster; by the petty, point-scoring conduct of political debate in both Parliament and media; by the short-term, parochial horizons of so much policy making; and by the withered notion of citizenship and participation in British political culture as a whole.[1]

Panel 22

British Politics and Public Disillusionment

In April–May 1995 the Joseph Rowntree Reform Trust commissioned MORI to conduct a State of the Nation opinion poll. A representative sample of 1,758 people were asked their views on the governance of Britain. The survey, which updated similar polls in 1973 and 1991, revealed a high and increasing level of disillusionment with the processes of British politics. When asked their opinion on 'the present system of governing Britain', the responses were as follows:

	1973	1991	1995
The present system of governing Britain...			
'Works extremely well' or 'Mainly works well'	48%	33%	22%
'Could be improved quite a lot' or			
'Needs a great deal of improvement'	49%	63%	76%
Don't know	4%	5%	3%

The 1995 British Social Attitudes survey (with a sample size of around 3,500) records an increasing mistrust of politicians. Respondents were asked how much they 'trust[ed] British governments of *any* party to place the needs of the nation above the interests of their own political party'. The results, with comparisons with previous similar surveys, were as follows:

	1986	1991	1994
Governments place needs of the nation above interests of party...			
'Just about always' or 'Most of the time'	38%	33%	24%
'Only some of the time' or 'Almost never'	57%	63%	73%

A new question in 1994 asked people whether they trusted 'politicians of any party to tell the truth when in a tight corner'. Just 9% of people said Yes.

In 1995 the think tank DEMOS published a report into the attitudes and values of young people aged 18–34, drawing on both quantitative (the British Household Panel study and MORI's *Socioconsult* survey) and qualitative (focus groups) data. The report found that many young people cared about environmental issues, famine, animal rights and HIV/AIDS; but few were interested in expressing these concerns through formal politics. People under 25 are four times less likely to be registered to vote than any other age group, less likely to join a political party, and less likely to be otherwise politically active. Only 43% of young people aged 18–24 voted at the last election.

Sources: MORI State of the Nation survey for the Joseph Rowntree Reform Trust, published in *British Public Opinion* (MORI newsletter), June 1995; J Curtice and R Jowell, 'The Sceptical Electorate' in R Jowell *et al* (eds), *British Social Attitudes: The 12th Report* (Aldershot: Dartmouth Publishing, 1995); H Wilkinson and G Mulgan, *Freedom's Children: Work, Relationships and Politics for 18–34 year olds in Britain Today* (London: Demos, 1995).

No Roads, New Politics
By ALARM UK

Nowhere has the disillusionment with current political structures been more evident than in the protest movement against roadbuilding that has sprung up over the last decade. The movement has reflected the growing insecurities of the middle classes, the terrible frustration of the deep-green environmentalists as well as the bitter anger of the dispossessed. These different strands have come together in what *The Economist* called 'the classless protest' to force a fundamental change in British transport policy.

The previous method of fighting road schemes – through Public Inquiries – proved markedly unsuccessful. For decades people opposing a destructive road scheme were conned by the Department of Transport into believing that, if they made carefully-crafted arguments at the Public Inquiry, they had a chance of preventing the road being built. Invariably, the public lost. In response the past decade has seen 'Middle England', which once regarded itself as the political establishment, form a loose, if tacit, alliance with the deep-greens and the penniless to fight a massive roads programme. Local groups campaigned 'on their own territory': using the media; organising colourful street stunts; producing sound transport alternatives; building up support in their communities; and then, for a handful of them, spectacular direct action.

Direct action of itself has not stopped a road; and by themselves the direct action protesters at around a dozen sites across the country would have been marginalised by the Government. But, in conjunction with the 250 or so local groups, many of them having taken on the Department of Transport and won, a transport policy has been overturned. From outwith established political structures. With negligible direct help from the main political parties. An indication of what 'people power' can achieve. But equally, a clear sign that current political structures are not meeting the concerns of so many people from all walks of life.

The failure of British politics to address the issues raised in this book attests to the problem. The environmental crisis and the new threats to international security, the changes to the global economic order, the impact of rising inequality on social cohesion and crime in Britain, the likelihood of achieving 'full employment', the role of local community organisations – these barely figure in national political debate, let alone policy. The mass media must take a substantial portion of the blame for this too. Political journalism is dominated by the set-piece rituals and minute conflicts of party politics at Westminster, its language and concerns both reflecting and influencing those of the professional politicians. Too rarely is attention focused

Witness Box 21

Sustainable Development and the Political System
*By Friends of the Earth**

For years, opinion polls have recorded rising public concern over a wide range of environmental problems. But when the parties go to the people seeking a mandate to govern, the environmental anxieties and demands of the electorate are ignored. Buttressed by the inbuilt biases of Britain's simple majority voting system, politicians from Left and Right feel comfortable if just a dash of green – a bit more pollution control here, a splash of habitat protection there – tinges their grey manifesto promises.

But progressing towards sustainability means addressing the root cause of environmental degradation: the dominant political orthodoxy which promotes continuous growth in consumption as a panacea for society's ills. Society must answer some tough questions. How high should energy prices rise to deter wasteful energy use, without penalising the poor? How can Britain's disproportionately high pollution rates and over-consumption of natural resources be reduced to globally equitable standards? As the VAT on fuel debacle showed, 'elected dictatorships' are not very good at either debating or resolving questions like these. Properly representative government is far more likely to do so.

Friends of the Earth is now convinced that an electoral system based on proportional representation is a fundamental requirement if we are to become an environmentally sustainable nation.

But more is needed to encourage citizens to act on their own environmental responsibilities. We believe that the state should guarantee all citizens inalienable environmental rights: rights, for example, to enjoy clean air, pure water, unadulterated food and uncontaminated land. Individuals and groups should be able to take both companies and government departments to court when these rights are violated. With such fundamental rights established in law, we believe individual citizens are far more likely to accept their own responsibilities to pollute and consume less.

New institutional arrangements in central and local government will be required if government is to fulfil its own sustainability obligations. Environmental protection, resource conservation and pollution control must now become the active mandate of all government departments, not just the Department of the Environment. To ensure this, we need a Ministry for the Environment and Natural Resources as powerful as the Treasury and the Foreign and Commonwealth Office, able to set policy restrictions and define opportunities for the rest of Whitehall and ensure that policies for sustainability are integrated across government.

*for England, Wales and Northern Ireland

on the world outside: on news from other parts of the globe – particularly outside Brussels and Washington – and on the variety of global forces and local experience that influence ordinary life for the majority of citizens.

The failure of the political system to address the problems of the real world breeds in most people simply apathy and disillusionment. But it may not always do so. In recent years Britain has seen an upsurge of popular protest, on issues such the poll tax, road building, animal welfare and the Criminal Justice Act. This is the unsurprising consequence of a political system which gives little opportunity for public participation and is unresponsive to new concerns. Most recent activity has been non-violent. But as urban riots continue occasionally to show, feelings of political powerlessness may lead to less accommodating forms of protest. Repressing dissent by law, the predominant approach of the Criminal Justice Act itself, is hardly an adequate response.

The Components of Reform

For Real World the importance of renewing democracy in Britain stems not only from its intrinsic benefits – a society with a vibrant democracy is a healthy society – but from its instrumental value. Put simply, sustainability and social justice, in this country or internationally, will not be achieved through the current form of the British political system. There are three grounds for this conclusion.

First, the issues which face Britain and the world today are complex, and will be politically difficult to manage. Some of them are unfamiliar; they require an understanding of changes presently occurring (environmental, social and economic) which have received very little debate up to now. They will need some very tough political choices to be made – on trade-offs between income growth, taxation and the provision of social goods, for example; or on required levels of environmental protection in conditions of uncertainty. This will require a seriousness and depth of political debate which present political institutions (including in this both Westminster and the mass media) seem largely incapable of providing. A restructuring of the form of politics – towards a system more open to new ideas and information, more responsive to the outside world, less ritually adversarial and more interested in investigation and persuasion – would seem to be a prerequisite for an improvement in its content.

Second, sustainability and social justice require a renewal of democracy because they require government. In recent years the promotion of markets as the best way of making decisions and allocating resources in

Witness Box 22

Poverty and Democracy
By Scottish Education and Action for Development (Sead)

There is more to democracy than the occasional chance to vote. There is more to poverty than a lack of the basic requirements for life. That the two are inextricably linked is not always acknowledged. It is however no accident that a political agenda set by those whose perspectives have been formed more by privilege than privation fails so often to reflect the priorities of the poor. In the circumstances it is no wonder that participation in formal democratic structures holds little attraction for those who live on the margins.

It would be wrong however to confuse this lack of engagement as evidence of wide-spread apathy. Rather it can be interpreted as rejection of a system which has failed to deliver the goods, in favour of the development of the practical skills, tactics and new models of organisation which can bring more control to disadvantaged groups and communities. Dynamism, commitment and imagination characterise local action world-wide. They are qualities which should be brought to two critical debates taking place today: the debate on sustainable development and the debate on the crisis of democracy.

Development which wreaks havoc on the lives of the poor in the short or long term is not sustainable. Reforms which simply overhaul institutions rather than create mechanisms for popular participation will not of themselves produce a democratic model for the next century.

Sead's work on poverty and democracy – 'Shifting the Balance: People, Power and Participation' – has provided a forum for activists from both the North and the South of the world to apply their talents to issues of development and democracy. Their experience, expertise and insights are crucial to ending a system where, both locally and globally, it is too often the wrong people asking the wrong questions and coming up with the wrong answers.

society has been accompanied by a belittling of government. Since government is identified with bureaucracy, inefficiency and the pursuit of vested interests, the purpose of politics, it is thought, should be to create less of it. In this context it is unsurprising that the democratic legitimacy of government has been of little concern.

As we have argued throughout this book, market forces are not capable of dealing with the critical problems now facing Britain and the world. They do not take account of environmental externalities; they do not generate sufficient employment to ensure social cohesion; they do not provide social goods; they do not reduce poverty, either domestically or overseas. Achieving all of these objectives requires deliberate and specific interventions by government. None of these conclusions imply opposition to markets. Markets must however operate within the constraints imposed by public decisions made for the common good. The market should be servant to society, not master.

But this in turn means that government is important; and that the legitimacy of government is central to its effectiveness in securing public goods. The goals of sustainability and social justice require new forms of economic intervention, regulation, taxation and public spending. Moreover they require these not just at a national level but internationally, and indeed locally. It is inconceivable that government will be able to secure the necessary powers unless the public in turn feel they have power over government. Government must be seen to be open to public influence and participation, to be accountable and responsive. It must be seen to be acting in the public interest, not vested interests. It must be seen to be capable of taking the longer-term and the wider view which the market cannot. These requirements are all too rarely met by the current institutions and processes of British politics.

Third, and consequently, the legitimacy of government implies a new relationship between state and individual. Sustainability and social justice will require new responsibilities of citizenship. Short-term economic gratification will have to give way to a broader perspective, in which the impacts of current actions on future generations, on the global ecosystem and on countries overseas will have to be taken into account. Higher taxation may be called for, as the price of public goods and social cohesion. Changes in lifestyle may be required – such as reduced use of the private car – in order to meet environmental imperatives. It is difficult to see responsibilities such as these being accepted without concomitant rights being guaranteed: the right to know; the right to judicial redress for harms committed; the right to participate in decision making. Translated into law these become the formal and inalienable rights of citizenship, rather than the vague and contingent rights of political subjects. If people are being asked to reassess their own political and economic relationship with others it would seem imperative for the constitution of the country to give them a guaranteed stake in the political system, making it not merely properly accountable to but representative of them. If it is clear that people belong to the political community they are surely more likely to respond as if they do.

Or rather, political *communities*, in the plural. For one of the most important implications of the sustainability and social justice agendas – and indeed, of public disillusionment – is the recognition of the importance of different levels of government. The idea that sovereignty can or should rest solely at the level of the nation state is simply obsolete in today's world.

Political power needs to be diffused: both upwards and downwards from the national level. Upwards, the processes of economic globalisation make the building of effective supranational institutions inevitable. Global sustainability and security require the regulation and management of international trade and finance and the control of transnational corporations. It is only through international institutions that these can be achieved.

The European Union is the essential starting point, since it already has governmental powers. But as current debates demonstrate – and not just in Britain – the legitimacy of the European Union is undermined by its lack of democracy. The evolution amongst the peoples of Europe of a genuinely European identity over the last two decades provides an unprecedented opportunity to build a democratic community at supranational level, by rebalancing the powers of the European Parliament, Council of Ministers and Commission. The EU has been a powerful promoter of the growth model, particularly in the development of the Single Market and in external trade policy. But it has also, in the social and environmental fields, done rather more to address the problems of this model than national government. Much of what we have argued in this book will require implementation, or at least support, at European level. The democratisation of European institutions is therefore almost certainly necessary if actions in pursuit of sustainability and social justice are to be taken.

Beyond Europe, the Bretton Woods institutions – the International Monetary Fund, World Bank and now the World Trade Organisation – need urgent reform. Further management of the global economy in pursuit of simple trade liberalisation and market deregulation can only lead to increasing environmental degradation and poverty and therefore to greater

Local Agenda 21 – Participation in Developing Sustainability
By the United Nations Association

One of the key outcomes from the Earth Summit in 1992 was the global action plan for sustainable development, Agenda 21. Agenda 21 calls local authorities throughout the world to 'consult with their communities' to develop their own 'Local Agenda 21'. Over 200 councils throughout the UK have taken up this challenge.

There is no simple template. Many have moved on from the traditional adversarial approach of British planning law to adopt a more open process that allows local people to raise their own concerns and needs. Whilst environmental groups have often been among the first to get involved, they are being joined by a range of community and social action groups looking for answers to such problems as crime, racism, poverty and social exclusion. The very idea of 'the environment' is being re-examined and presented as a concern for everyone, not just for the usual activists.

The involvement of other sectors or 'stakeholders' also presents new challenges. Businesses and statutory bodies find themselves sitting round the table with community organisations they may previously only have confronted, looking for economic development options that also improve social equity.

Local authorities themselves are having to adopt new ways of working. Some are using environmental management systems to put their own houses in order. Many have Local Agenda 21 teams bringing together staff from different departments, offering new perspectives on how local government can work to meet local needs.

The real challenge is to move from consultation to active public and stakeholder participation, with authorities delegating power to community-based fora. In many places the structures are already in place. As Local Agenda 21s turn into local sustainability plans, they reveal that sustainable development is not just about environmental protection and the meeting of social needs. It's also about the revival of democracy itself.

113

international insecurity. A new 'constitutional settlement' is needed, involving greater institutional openness and accountability, larger representation for the developing countries, and a commitment to sustainability, the eradication of poverty and enhanced security. A new, stable international financial order is a priority. Proposals for an Economic Security Council and other reforms to the United Nations and its agencies made by the Commission on Global Governance merit serious examination.[2]

Some powers must therefore be devolved upwards. But this makes it even more important that other powers are devolved downwards, from the

A Charter for Constitutional Reform
By *Charter* 88

Charter 88 believes that Britain needs a written constitution which will vest power where it belongs – in the people. Our demands would give Britain the structures of a modern, power-sharing democracy, anchored in the idea of universal citizenship.

A Bill of Rights is needed because the citizens of the UK have no guaranteed rights, only permissions which the state has granted and the state may take away. Guaranteed rights symbolise a truly democratic culture. We need a fair voting system of proportional representation because millions of us are currently denied a basic right – that each vote should count equally.

Our system of government is centralised and unaccountable. A party with a parliamentary majority wields unbridled power. Governments can exercise Crown Prerogative without consulting Parliament, and the use of secondary legislation and statutory instruments has increased enormously over recent years. The House of Commons must be reformed because Parliament is unrepresentative, inaccessible, hostile to women and to minorities, and cannot hold government to account. Its adversarial structure is an embarrassment to any advocate of democracy. An Upper House filled by heredity and patronage is an indefensible anachronism. A democratically elected Upper House would act as a revising Chamber and a check against abuses of power by the Commons.

We need devolution of power because Britain is one of the most centralised states in Europe. Scotland and Wales are distinctive nations within the UK. Yet they are currently governed like provinces of Whitehall, by a governing party which in recent years has had the support of less than a third of their voters. Both nations should have parliaments of their own. Independence for local government is also required. This is the level of government most accessible to the citizen. Yet its functions are being hived off to centrally-appointed quangos and it depends on central government for 85% of its funding.

Without freedom of information the citizens of this country do not have the right to know what is done in their name. Nor do victims of miscarriages of justice have an automatic right of access to the courts or right to compensation. We need a guaranteed right of redress for all state abuse. At the same time, reform of the judiciary is needed to give improved accountability, a better balance in the selection and appointment of judges and a guarantee of independence.

A written constitution will not deliver what is not already in our hearts and minds. It won't do the work of citizenship for us. But it can help open the way for a genuinely living democracy.

level of the nation state to Britain's individual nations, regions and localities. Indeed, almost certainly, the one cannot be achieved without the other. Only if government is as close to the people as possible will it have the legitimacy to act on their collective behalf. As the processes of globalisation gather pace, so a simultaneous move towards the local will act as counterweight.

Over the last decade and a half much of local government in Britain has tried hard to work towards social justice and sustainability. Major efforts have been directed at local economic regeneration, community development, combating poverty and environmental improvement. But these have been consistently hampered by the centralised nature of the British constitution, which allows national government to remove resources from local government at will, and which prevents local authorities – as statutory bodies with only delegated powers – from taking the measures they deem necessary to deal with local issues.

Subsidiarity should therefore be taken seriously: not just as the principle of appropriate division of powers between Europe and national governments, but between central and local government. Yet neither is this enough. For local government can be bureaucratic and unresponsive too. Councils can also devolve power: both by making their own processes more open and participative and by giving local communities the opportunity to manage themselves. It is at local level that most people naturally want and feel able to participate in political life: in public debate, and in the making and management of decisions which affect their lives. It is therefore at local level – from bottom-up – that a fully democratic society is constructed. The role played in this by voluntary and community groups is crucial, empowering people whose voices are otherwise unheard, enabling participation in wider political processes. Strengthening the role and capacity of local community groups is therefore an essential part of democratic reform.

In this way the renewal of democracy in Britain is not simply about redistributing power between levels of government. It is also about rejuvenating our political culture. Democracy needs open debate and freedom of information. A plural and enquiring press, genuinely open to political argument, is absolutely essential to this. Unfortunately, as the unwillingness to engage with the issues raised in this book demonstrates, it would be difficult to claim that this is what we have today – particularly as media ownership continues to become more concentrated. For the same reason, it is vital to democracy that a culture of public service broadcasting on television and radio is maintained.

Alongside this, a rejuvenated political culture requires a belief in participation. This is more than voting or public consultation on policy, important (and currently limited) though these are. It is about strengthening civil society in the processes of government. In the modern world of rapid transmission of information, global economic forces and far-reaching cultural change, government must involve all sectors of society in both the making of policy and in its implementation. At local level, participatory and partnership initiatives such as Local Agenda 21 are growing in number, demonstrating imagination and vitality in the task of widening public involvement (see Witness Box 23). At national level too Britain needs a vibrant civil society to debate, to think through and to make possible the new imperatives of environmental sustainability and social justice.

Conclusions:
The Politics of the Real World

7

Towards an Alternative Model

As we approach the new century, it has become increasingly clear that the model of economic and social progress which has dominated the second half of the present one no longer works. The problems of environmental degradation, global poverty and domestic inequality have begun to threaten, even to overwhelm, the gains which have been made. At risk is the security of nations and the quality of human life – even for those who are the apparent beneficiaries of progress. As we have tried to show in this book, the failure of the model lies not just in the existence of these problems, or even their increase. It lies in the way in which current patterns of economic growth, based on the expansion of market forces, are themselves their cause. The model is ultimately self-defeating.

Its failures in turn point the way to an alternative approach. It is such an approach which underlies the policy proposals contained in the separate chapters of this book.

Any alternative model must start by addressing the unquestioned pursuit of economic growth. Over the last 50 years growth has become the main objective of politics, regarded not just as the source of wealth creation but as the automatic solution to all other problems. But from each of the substantive fields of concern covered in this document – environmental degradation, global poverty, inequality, unemployment and quality of life in Britain – a different picture has emerged. This is that economic growth *per se* does not achieve wider objectives; on the contrary, current patterns of growth actually generate many of the problems.

Growth does provide resources which can pay for some social and environmental improvements. It is essential that the incomes and material living standards of the poor, both in developing countries and in the UK, are raised. But growth of itself will not reduce environmental degradation: on the contrary, because of the central relationship between current patterns of growth and the major environmental problems we face, more of such growth will make them worse. Growth of itself will not reduce poverty – as the experience of the last two decades has demonstrated, both within Britain and in the world as a whole. Growth of itself is not even the key to cutting unemployment: the targeting of economic expansion in particular sectors is what matters. It is not growth which creates social cohesion: again, the inequality arising from current patterns of growth only contributes to the decline in community and the social problems which follow. Neither is it growth from which comes the quality of life: in particular, raising private incomes when what are needed are social goods can only make society overall poorer.

The problem here lies in one of the most long-standing assumptions of contemporary politics. This is that 'social and environmental issues' are essentially questions of distribution. The economy produces wealth: this can then be redistributed to alleviate poverty, improve the environment, and so on. But where *the processes of production themselves* are the causes of these problems, this approach is doomed to failure. Concentrating effort on increasing production in order to have more resources available to redistribute only adds to the problems with which such distribution is meant to deal.

The priority given to economic growth in political and economic life therefore needs to be changed. Instead of economic policy overriding all others, with wider objectives relegated to mere derivatives of growth, these objectives should be regarded as the priorities themselves. Not just social and environmental but (crucially) economic policy should then be addressed directly to them. Domestically, the new direct objectives should start with achieving environmental sustainability, reducing inequality and poverty, and increasing and redistributing employment and work. In general, the primary aim should be, not private income growth, but improvements in the quality of life; that is, in the overall wellbeing of individuals and in the social and cultural development of society as a whole. Internationally, our first objectives should be to eradicate poverty and to protect environmental resources, so as to ensure security, both within and between nations.

None of these objectives preclude growth: this is not an argument against raising incomes. Indeed, we suspect that increasing environmental investment and expanding employment will generate growth, though we cannot say it will be the fastest growth potentially available, or that it will be directed principally into average personal consumption. It *is* an argument against regarding the raising of incomes as the first purpose of government and the principal measure of its success. If poverty declines, environmental quality improves and people feel safer, then we are better off, and government should be regarded as having done well – even if GDP is not rising as fast as it otherwise might have done.

In rejecting the pursuit of growth *per se* as its primary objective, an alternative approach must also modify the dominant model's means. As again each of the issues addressed in this book shows, free market forces cannot play the role required of them. Environmental degradation is an 'externality' of unregulated markets, which do not register and therefore do not prevent costs being imposed on others. Throughout the world poverty follows from economic marginalisation, as market forces withdraw demand, remove resources from and dictate prices to those in less fortunate geographic areas and economic positions. Economic globalisation uproots communities and destroys settled cultures, in Britain as throughout the world; a process then reinforced by the motivation of self-interest encouraged by the market ideology. Improving the quality of life requires investment in social goods, where reliance on market forces directs spending into private consumption.

Again, the crucial realisation is that these outcomes are not incidental by-products of market forces, but central, predictable consequences of them. The problems caused must be addressed by alternative means.

This requires government. It is not markets themselves to which we take exception, but the abdication of democratic decision making to the socially and environmentally damaging outcomes of overall market forces.

Markets are essential. But they must be shaped in the interests of society, not vice versa. It is simply not the case that a globalising economy must reduce all national economies to the lowest common denominator of deregulated markets; as observation of the differences between (say) Germany, Japan, the US, Sweden, the UK and Singapore reveals, different societies can shape their economies and social structures very differently.

In place of market forces, solutions to the problems discussed in this book require societies as a whole to make decisions about their objectives: at national, international and local levels. They then require governments with the mandate and the power to influence and constrain market forces to generate these chosen outcomes. To do this governments have many tools at their disposal: law, taxation, public expenditure, incentive, persuasion. But the crucial role is the democratic one: the ability of government to pursue that common good which eludes unconstrained markets.

Markets fail; but so do governments. No-one could say that governments always pursue the common good: they can spawn unresponsive bureaucracies and may be captured by vested interests. Contrary to the general assumption of political debate, however, markets and governments do not exhaust the possibility of social organisation. The third, crucial leg of the stool is civil society: the autonomous activities of citizens and their voluntary associations in economic, political and cultural life. As we have argued in this book, voluntary and community-based groups must play a central part in any strategy of renewal. The strength of this sector limits and influences both markets and state. It is in civil society that ethical values and ideas of the common good find clearest expression, articulated in public debate and embodied in voluntary associations. Such values and ideas are the moral source of government. Increasingly too, as the persistent debate about business ethics attests, they are having their impact on corporate life.

The strengthening and growth of civil society are at the heart of what Real World means by 'democratic renewal'. We have argued here that democratic reform is a central component of the wider approach we seek. We do not see how the challenges facing this country and the world can be properly articulated or addressed within the constraints of Britain's present political system. As its lack of response to these challenges itself demonstrates, the processes of politics in Britain are too archaic, too short-term and too closed to permit the responses necessary – or even the debate. The rejuvenation of democracy will require far-reaching reform in the institutions of politics and government. But such reform must be founded on a new culture of participation, and this can only arise 'from the bottom up', from civil society.

Real World and British Politics

Real World is in itself a manifestation of this process. We seek not merely to argue for democratic revitalisation, but to reflect it. In attempting to raise the issues of sustainability, social justice and democratic renewal we hope to force concerns arising from within civil society onto the agenda of debate in the institutions and media of British politics.

It will no doubt be argued that our concerns are not shared by the British people at large. The electorate does not want to know about people in the Third World, or the poor in Britain. Environmental concern is shallow, easily outweighed by the continuing attractions of material consumption. Democratic reform is a minority pursuit. Above all the suggestions that income taxes may have to rise, and that disposable incomes for average households may not rise, seem designed to repel widespread support. In the 'culture of contentment' reported by J K Galbraith,[1] the majority are happy with their low taxes and increasingly private consumption; they will not be moved by the needs of a wider community.

We do not agree. We have made an unashamedly ethical case: that the harms caused by environmental degradation, global poverty, and unemployment and inequality in Britain are intolerable in themselves. They profoundly damage people's lives. But it has also become clear, throughout this book, that such damage cannot be confined to those directly hurt. In each case the problems we have discussed have begun to affect the wellbeing of people in the UK – or now threaten to do so. As environmental degradation causes ill-health and loss of treasured places and fear for our children's future, so the effects of poverty emerge in crime and anti-social behaviour and the insistent sense that society is breaking down. As the globalisation and deregulation of markets makes even middle class jobs feel vulnerable, so the combination of rising poverty, worsening environments, migration and political conflict makes international security ever more fragile.

This is the interdependence of the world in the 21st century. The problems we have discussed seep inexorably across boundaries – those of nations, residential areas, economic and social class. More and more it is becoming clear that it is in almost everybody's interest, whether more affluent or less, in the rich world or poor, to address them. This will mean spending resources, of course, and such resources must come primarily from the more affluent. But not spending them can only mean allowing the problems, and their effects, to get worse.

The latter approach has its advocates. From a dominant strand of current US politics (where social breakdown has gone much further), and from parts of the right in Europe, comes the apparently tempting offer of safety through insulation. Average middle-income voters can be protected from the social decay of their own society and the poverty and conflict of the world around them: not by reducing these problems, by taking responsibility for the wider community; but by withdrawing from it into the bunker of narrow self-interest: reducing taxes, cutting public services, ending overseas aid, restricting immigration, erecting security walls (metaphorical and physical) between themselves and the imagined danger outside. In the short term, this approach looks cheaper; to the individual middle-income voter it seems to offer a private way out, not dependent on the uncertain cooperation of others. But it is doomed to failure. In an interdependent world there is no security behind protective walls; without expression or solution the tensions and conflicts generated by an unequal society and world can only become more severe, and they will not be held outside. Meanwhile, inside the walls, people will live increasingly fearful, narrow lives, hurt by anxiety and mistrust of others.

Most people in Britain, we believe, will regard this prospect as appalling, and will wish to avoid it. The alternative seems to us inescapable. Responsibility for the whole community – globally, and within the UK – must be accepted by all. The problems we face must be reduced by common action, not shut away. Though there will be financial costs, the return in terms of genuine security and the quality of community life will be far higher. This is in everyone's interest, even that of the reasonably affluent who will have to pay the larger share.

In fact we do not believe that the two appeals we make – to both morality and self-interest – can be kept apart. For a society which upholds ethical principles is itself for many people a better place in which to live.

Contrary to the cynical view which pervades modern politics, many people in Britain do care about the morality of their society, and wish to act upon it. The evidence for this is found in many places: in the continuing rise of green consumerism and ethical investment; in the moral foundation of recent political protest, such as over animal welfare, the loss of country-side to road building, the Brent Spar; in the growing debate on corporate ethics, exemplified by the public response to Shell's involvement in Ogoniland in Nigeria. It has been revealed in the public outcry over executive share options and 'top people's pay' – not the 'politics of envy', this, but a simpler one of fairness, opposed to greed. It is found in the ever-present vitality and huge participation rates of Britain's voluntary sector.

For most people, ethical motivations of these kinds reflect a desire to live in a moral society: one which cares for its less fortunate members, for its natural environment and for the idea of community. They reflect the feeling which many people who have not themselves been hurt – who may even have done personally very well – have had in recent years, that there is something deeply uncomfortable about living in a society which tolerates homelessness and rising poverty, racial discrimination and environmental destruction. We have been told in these years that what matters is personal consumption and rising material living standards. It seems to us that many people recognise that there is more to life than this: more to their own personal development, and more to building a good society.

In fact the evidence suggests a very widespread feeling that something is wrong with Britain and British politics. Public attitude surveys show, for example, how deep are anxieties about environmental degradation, and about the loss of community and growth of crime. Across society there is concern that mass unemployment is destroying the hopes and prospects for young people. All these factors contribute to a widespread fear about the future. We have noted the evidence of public disillusionment with politics. It would be surprising if this were entirely unrelated to the failure of the British political system to address the issues we have raised here.

We therefore do believe that there is a political audience for Real World's analysis and approach. Not all of it will be accepted; some of our conclusions may at the moment be politically unpalatable. But it is one of the functions of political leadership to bring difficult issues into public debate. The challenges facing Britain and the world are real enough; and addressing them is the first imperative.

In this book we have set out the broad directions of change we believe to be required. But we do not claim to have all the solutions. We recognise the political dilemmas in what we advocate. We know, for example, that there is a potential conflict between the desire for increasing consumption in both Northern and Southern societies and the imperative of limiting environmental impacts. We do not know whether improvements in environmental efficiency will come fast and large enough, or perceptions of the 'quality of life' can be adjusted sufficiently to allow for reduced material consumption. We know that the requirement to redistribute resources from North to South is limited by the need to maintain political support in the North; particularly between the interests of workers in the North and workers in the South when markets are opened up. We recognise that there is a conflict between higher taxation and the desire for more personal consumption, and between government intervention in the economy and the maintenance of efficient, internationally competitive enterprises.

For these reasons, among others, we acknowledge how difficult will be the political process in any movement for reform. But the crucial task is to get the issues into the open for honest and realistic discussion. If Real World can do this, we shall have achieved our primary objective.

A Vision for the New Century

At a time of political malaise and widespread despair, Real World thus represents a movement of hope and belief that the world can be changed. Our vision is of a world in which poverty is progressively eradicated, diverse and sustainable natural environments are maintained and population growth slows; in which rising incomes and improved standards of living in the South are matched by reduced material consumption and improved quality of life in the North; in which women and men throughout the world are equally able to achieve their full potential; in which military spending is reduced to the minimum necessary and social development flourishes.

Our vision is of a Britain in which a reduction in inequality and an increase in both collective and individual security provides everyone with the opportunity to fulfil their potential; in which greater social cohesion strengthens both national and local communities; in which the diversity and wealth of the natural environment is maintained; in which cultural diversity is celebrated; in which the improved provision of social goods raises everybody's quality of life even as material consumption falls to sustainable levels; in which a thriving democracy allows all to participate.

If Real World's vision looks radical this is a measure of how feeble the idea of political purpose in Britain has now become. We are convinced it is achievable. Continuation on the present path offers only further decline – perhaps even catastrophe. The dawn of a new century marks an appropriate time for change.

References

Chapter 1

1. See for example the MORI 'State of the Nation' survey for the Joseph Rowntree Reform Trust, May 1995, reported in *British Public Opinion* (MORI Newsletter), June 1995, and J Curtice and R Jowell 'The Sceptical Electorate' in R Jowell *et al* (eds), *British Social Attitudes: The 12th Report* (Aldershot: Dartmouth Publishing, 1995). See also Panel 22, page 106.
2. This includes members, volunteers, subscribers and identified financial supporters. It does not include members of organisations affiliated to Real World member organisations. It will include some double-counting (individuals belonging to more than one organisation).

Chapter 2

1. See for example F Fukuyama, *The End of History and the Last Man* (London: Penguin 1992).
2. United Nations Development Programme, *Human Development Report 1994* (Oxford: Oxford University Press, 1994), p135; United Nations 1989 *Report on the World Situation* (New York: UN, 1989), p39. Although the percentage of poor people has declined, this has not kept pace with population growth.
3. An example is the Index of Sustainable Economic Welfare (ISEW), which adjusts GDP by a number of economic and social factors. See T Jackson and N Marks, *Measuring Sustainable Economic Welfare* (London: New Economics Foundation and Stockholm Environment Institute, 1994). ISEW is explained further and illustrated in Panel 19 on p82. See also R Hawkins, J Webb and D Corry, 'The New Economy Wellbeing Index', *New Economy*, Vol 3, No 1, 1996.
4. United Nations Children's Fund, *Annual Report 1994* (New York: UNICEF, 1994), p6.

Chapter 3

1. M Thatcher, speech to the Royal Society, 22 September 1988.
2. *Financial Times*, 25 March 1995. See also Greenpeace, *Climate Change and the Insurance Industry* (London: Greenpeace, 1993).
3. World Health Organisation, *Our Planet, Our Health: Report of the WHO Commission on Health and Environment* (Geneva: WHO, 1992); Friends of the Earth, *Prescription for Change: Health and the Environment* (London: FoE, 1995).
4. See for example M Tolba *et al* (eds), *The World Environment 1972–92* (London: Chapman & Hall/UN Environment Programme, 1992); Department of the Environment, *Digest of Environmental Protection and Water Statistics No 17 1995* (London: HMSO, 1995); L Brown *et al* (eds), *Vital Signs 1995–96* (London:

Earthscan, 1995), and previous reports.

5.   See for example World Bank, World Development Report 1992: Development and the Environment (Washington DC: World Bank, 1992); World Resources Institute, World Resources 1994–5 (Washington DC: WRI, 1994) and previous annual reports; L Brown et al (eds), State of the World 1995 (London: Earthscan, 1995) and previous annual reports.

6.   M Parry, Climate Change and World Agriculture (London: Earthscan, 1990); Commonwealth Secretariat, Climate Change: Meeting the Challenge (London: Commonwealth Secretariat, 1989). For a summary, see K Watkins, The Oxfam Poverty Report (Oxford: Oxfam, 1995), pp151–3. See also in general World Bank, World Development Report 1992, op cit.

7.   B Boardman, Fuel Poverty: From Cold Homes to Affordable Warmth (London: Belhaven/Wiley, 1991). This figure is now estimated as 8 million, given the rise in the number of means-tested benefit claimants (Hansard, 1 April 1993, col 492) and the lack of progress on domestic insulation (B Boardman, personal communication).

8.   P Townsend and N Davidson (eds)/M Whitehead, Inequalities in Health: The Black Report, The Health Divide (London: Penguin, 1992).

9.   H M Government, Sustainable Development: The UK Strategy, Cmnd 2426 (London: HMSO, 1994).

10. UNICEF, The State of the World's Children 1994 (Oxford: Oxford University Press, 1994), p35.

11. UN Population Fund, The State of World Population 1994 (New York: UNFPA, 1994).

12. International Conference on Population and Development: Programme of Action (New York: UNPFA, 1994); United Nations, World Population Prospects: The 1994 Revision (New York: UN, 1995); P Harrison, The Third Revolution (London: Penguin, 1993), p329.

13. P Harrison, The Third Revolution op cit, pp256–7; 'Consumption Patterns: The Driving Force of Environmental Stress', Research Paper No 3 prepared for the UN Conference on Environment and Development, Indira Gandhi Institute of Development Research, Bombay, 1991. Plus adjusted figures from UNICEF, The State of the World's Children 1994, op cit, p34.

14. IPCC, Climate Change: The IPCC Scientific Assessment (Cambridge: Cambridge University Press, 1990); UN Development Programme, Human Development Report 1994 op cit, p18.

15. OECD, Environmental Policies and Industrial Competitiveness (Paris: OECD, 1993); T Barker (ed), Green Futures for Economic Growth (Cambridge: Cambridge Econometrics, 1991); DRI et al, Potential Benefits of Integration of Environmental and Economic Policies (London: Graham and Trottman/Commission of the European Communities, 1994); M Jacobs, Green Jobs? The Employment Implications of Environmental Policy (Brussels: World Wide Fund for Nature, 1994).

16. OECD, Urban Transport and Sustainable Development (Paris: OECD, 1995);

R Tolley (ed), *The Greening of Urban Transport* (London: Belhaven, 1990). In an NOP poll in early 1995 64% of people wanted cars actively discouraged and urgent government intervention to stem car dependency (*Guardian*, 22 July 1995). See also G Stokes and B Taylor, 'Where Next for Transport Policy?' in R Jowell *et al* (eds) *British Social Attitudes: The 12th Report* (Aldershot: Dartmouth Publishing, 1995).

17. See World Bank, *World Development Report 1992* (Washington, DC: World Bank, 1992); L Brown *et al*, *Saving the Planet* (London: Earthscan, 1992).

18. Advisory Council on Business and the Environment, *Fifth Progress Report to and Response From the President of the Board of Trade and the Secretary of State for the Environment* (London: Department of the Environment, 1995), and Reports 1–4; Confederation of British Industry, *Environment Costs* (London: CBI, 1995).

19. See for example S Schmidheiny with the Business Council for Sustainable Development, *Changing Course* (Cambridge, Ma: MIT Press, 1992).

129

20. L Brown *et al*, *Saving the Planet op cit*; D Meadows *et al* (eds), *Beyond the Limits* (London: Earthscan, 1992).

Chapter 4

1. UN Development Programme, *Human Development Report 1994*, *op cit*, p135; World Health Organisation, *Bridging the Gaps*: The World Health Report 1995 (Geneva: WHO, 1995) pp1–6, 44; United Nations, 1989 *Report on the World Social Situation*, *op cit*, p39; UN Population Fund *State of World Population 1992* (New York: UNFPA, 1992), pp3–5.

2. World Bank, *World Data 1995* on CD-Rom (Washington DC: World Bank, 1995). The figures compare 1993 and 1963.

3. World Bank, *World Development Report 1992 op cit*.

4. G Cornia, *Macroeconomic Policy, Poverty Alleviation and Long-Term Development*: *Latin America in the 1990s* (New York: UNICEF Innocenti Papers, 1994).

5. World Bank, *World Development Report 1990: Poverty* (Washington DC: World Bank); UNDP, *Human Development Report 1994*, *op cit*.

6. W Brandt, *North-South: A Programme for Survival* (London: Pan, 1980).

7. World Bank, *Global Economic Prospects and Developing Countries* (Washington DC: World Bank, 1994).

8. World Bank, *The East Asian Miracle*, World Bank Policy Research Report (Oxford: Oxford University Press, 1995).

9. World Bank, *World Data 1995*, *op cit*.

10. UNDP, *Human Development Report 1994*, *op cit*, p65.

11. UNICEF, *State of the World's Children 1994*, *op cit*, p51; B Jackson, *Poverty and the Planet*, 2nd edn (London: Penguin, 1995).

12. I Elbadawi *et al*, 'World Bank Adjustment Lending and Economic Performance in Sub-Saharan Africa', World Bank Policy Research Working Paper, 1992; P Mosley and J Weeks, 'Has Recovery Begun? "Africa's Adjustment in the 1980s" Revisited', *World Development*, Vol 21, No 10, 1993, pp1583–1603;

A Sepehri, 'Back to the Future?', *Review of African Political Economy*, No 2, 1994, pp559–568. For a survey see K Watkins, *The Oxfam Poverty Report, op cit*.

13. World Bank, *The East Asian Miracle, op cit*, pp79-102.

14. UN Conference on Trade and Development, *World Investment Report 1994* (Geneva: UNCTAD, 1994).

15. E Kolodner, *Transnational Corporations: Impediments or Catalysts of Social Development?* (Geneva: UN Research Institute for Social Development, 1994); A Dwyer, *On the Line: Life on the US–Mexican Border* (London: Latin America Bureau, 1994).

16. 'Poverty is the father of dictatorship....' Dr Kofi Awoonor, Ghanaian Ambassador to the United Nations, quoted in UNICEF, *State of the World's Children 1994, op cit*, p33.

17. UN High Commissioner for Refugees, *The State of the World's Refugees* 1995 (Geneva: UNHCR, 1995), p247; UNHCR, *UNHCR by Numbers* (Geneva: UNHCR, 1995), p2.

18. UNHCR, collated in N Myers, 'Eco-refugees: A Crisis in the Making', *People and the Planet*, Vol 3, No 4, 1994, p7.

19. S Postel, *The Last Oasis: Facing Water Scarcity* (London: Earthscan, 1992).

20. *Observer*, 2 April 1995. See also T Homer-Dixon *et al*, 'Environmental Change and Violent Conflict', *Scientific American*, vol 268, no 2, 1993, pp16–23; N Myers, *Ultimate Security: The Environmental Basis of Political Stability* (New York: WW Norton, 1993).

21. N Myers, 'Environmental Refugees in a Globally Warmed World', *BioScience*, Vol 43, No 11, 1993, pp752–761.

22. UNDP, *Human Development Report 1994, op cit*, p54.

23. K Watkins, *The Oxfam Poverty Report, op cit*, p51.

24. A Wood, *North-South Trade, Employment and Inequality* (Oxford: Oxford University Press, 1993).

25. A Singh and A Zammit, 'Employment and Unemployment, North and South', in J Michie and J Grieve Smith (eds), *Managing the Global Economy* (Oxford: Oxford University Press, 1995).

26. See for example UN Conference on Trade and Development, UNCTAD *Trade and Development Report 1994* (Geneva: UNCTAD, 1994).

27. *Guardian*, 25 April 1995. Michael Camdessus was responding to a period of particular turbulence in the currency markets which saw a near-20% devaluation of the dollar against the Japanese yen.

28. OECD, OECD *Development Assistance Committee Report* (Paris: OECD, 1995).

29. Proposed by the Nobel Laureate economist James Tobin in UNDP, *Human Development Report 1994, op cit*, p70.

30. 'Financial Data Relating to NATO Defence', NATO Press Release, Brussels, 29 November 1995, Table 1 (figures for 1990); A Gore, *Earth in the Balance* (London: Earthscan, 1992), p304; L Freedman and E Karsh, *The Gulf Conflict* (London: Faber and Faber, 1995), p358.

31. UNDP, *Human Development Report* 1994, *op cit*, p77.
32. *Ibid*, p48.
33 *Ibid*, p9.

Chapter 5

1. Joseph Rowntree Foundation, *Inquiry Into Income and Wealth* (York: JRF, 1995). A full analysis is given in A Goodman and S Webb, *For Richer, For Poorer: The Changing Distribution of Income in the UK 1961–91* (London: Institute for Fiscal Studies, 1994).
2. A Atkinson *et al*, *Income Distribution in OECD Countries: Evidence from the Luxembourg Income Study* (Paris: OECD, 1995).
3. Joseph Rowntree Foundation, *Inquiry Into Income and Wealth*, *op cit*, Vol 1, pp15, 28–9; S Webb, 'Women's Incomes: Past, Present and Prospects', *Fiscal Studies*, Vol 14, No 4, pp14–36; Department of Social Security, *Households Below Average Income* 1979–1992/93 (London: DSS, 1995). For a survey see C Oppenheim and L Harker, *Poverty: The Facts* (London: Child Poverty Action Group, 1996).
4. B Boardman, *Fuel Poverty: From Cold Homes to Affordable Warmth*, *op cit*. This figure is now estimated as 8 million (see chapter 3, note 7).
5. See A Power and R Tunstall, *Swimming Against the Tide* (York: Joseph Rowntree Foundation, 1995); Bishops' Advisory Group on Urban Priority Areas, *Staying in the City* (London: Church House Publishing, 1995).
6. Central Statistical Office, NOMIS on-line database, December 1995.
7. Central Statistical Office, Labour Force Survey (August 1995) calculated in Unemployment Unit, *Working Brief*, No 71, February 1996. The extra numbers are arrived at by taking the 'Standard' Labour Force Survey (International Labour Organisation) measure of unemployment and adding other categories of people available for, but not seeking, work. See also Panel 17 on p73.
8. P Gregg and J Wadsworth, 'Making Work Pay', *New Economy*, Vol 2, No 4, 1995, pp210–213 (Labour Force Survey data); Joseph Rowntree Foundation, *Inquiry into Income and Wealth*, *op cit*, Vol 1, p23. Gregg and Wadsworth's paper updates the figures given in the Rowntree report.
9. Goodman and Webb, *For Richer and Poorer*, *op cit*.
10. Joseph Rowntree Foundation, *Inquiry into Income and Wealth*, *op cit*, Vol 1, p36.
11. D Corry and A Glyn, 'The Macroeconomics of Equality, Stability and Growth', in A Glyn and D Miliband (eds), *Paying for Inequality: The Economic Cost of Social Injustice* (London: Institute for Public Policy Research/Rivers Oram Press, 1994).
12. S Box, *Recession, Crime and Punishment* (London: Macmillan, 1987); J Hagan and R Peterson (eds); *Crime and Inequality* (Stanford, Ca: Stanford University Press, 1995).
13. M Hillman, *Children, Transport and the Quality of Life* (London: Policy Studies Institute, 1993).

14. D McNeish and H Roberts, *Playing It Safe* (London: Barnardo's, 1995).
15. A Beck and A Willis, *Crime and Security: Managing the Risk to Safe Shopping* (Leicester: Perpetuity Press, 1995).
16. Central Statistical Office, *United Kingdom National Accounts* 1984, p71 and 1995, p79 (London: HMSO, 1984, 1995). At constant 1990 prices, expenditure on police, prisons and law courts was £56.3 billion in 1974 and £110.4 billion in 1994.
17. National Asthma Campaign, from W Lenney *et al* 'The Burden of Paediatric Asthma', *European Respiratory Review*, Vol 4, No 18, 1994, pp49–62; D Strachan *et al* 'A National Survey of Asthma Prevalence, Severity and Treatment in Great Britain', *Archives of Disease in Childhood*, No 70, 1994, pp174–178; C Read (ed), *How Vehicle Pollution Affects Our Health*, Report of a Symposium held on 20 May 1994 (London: Ashden Trust, 1994); J Whitelegg *et al*, *Traffic and Health*, Environmental Epidemiology Research Unit, Lancaster University, 1993.
18. *Guardian*, 31 October 1995.
19. *Guardian*, 18 October 1995.
20. P Warr, *Work, Unemployment and Mental Health* (Oxford: Oxford University Press, 1987).
21. J Williamson, *Hard Labour: Britain's Longer Working Week* (London: TUC, 1995).
22. *Ibid*; Austin Knight, 'The Family Friendly Workplace', Survey Report, October 1995.
23. Eurobarometer Survey Series cited in A Oswald, 'Happiness and Economic Performance', mimeo, Centre for Economic Performance, London School of Economics, 1995. One example of such a measure of wellbeing is the Index of Sustainable Economic Welfare. See Panel 19 on p82.
24. See Barnardo's, *The Facts of Life: The Changing Face of Childhood* (London: Barnardo's, 1995).
25. See for example V Anderson, *Alternative Economic Indicators* (London: Routledge, 1991).
26. Cuts in these areas were announced at the time of the 1995 Budget.
27. See for example F Field MP, *Making Welfare Work* (London: Institute of Community Studies, 1995); R Dahrendorf *et al*, *Report on Wealth Creation and Social Cohesion in a Free Society* (London: The Commission on Wealth Creation & Social Cohesion, 1995); Help the Aged, *Coming Clean on Care Costs* (London: Help the Aged, 1995).
28. See for example J Robertson, *Benefits and Taxes: A Radical Strategy* (London: New Economics Foundation, 1994). The proposal for a Citizen's Income is explored in more detail in H Parker, *Instead of the Dole* (London: Routledge, 1989).
29. Joseph Rowntree Foundation, *Inquiry into Income and Wealth*, *op cit*.
30. OECD, *Revenue Statistics of OECD Member Countries* 1965–94 (Paris: OECD, 1995).

31. OECD, *Historical Statistics* (Paris: OECD, 1995), p71. The latest comparative figures available are for 1993. See also J Hills, *The Future of Welfare: A Guide to the Debate* (York: Joseph Rowntree Foundation, 1994).

32. OECD, *Economic Outlook* (Paris: OECD, June 1995), pA32

33. *Ibid*, p13.

34. See P Warr, P Jackson and M Banks, 'Unemployment and Mental Health: Some British Studies', *Journal of Social Issues*, Vol 44, pp47–68; A Clark and A Oswald, 'Unhappiness and Unemployment', *The Economic Journal*, Vol 104, May 1994, pp648–659.

35. Unemployment Unit, *Working Brief*, No 70, December 1995. This figure includes the cost of benefits, administration, redundancy funds and fore-gone tax revenues.

36. *Labour Market Trends*, January 1996, pS10.

37. P Hewitt, *About Time* (London: Institute for Public Policy Research / Rivers Oram Press, 1993).

38. For example, a 'parent wage', paid to mothers and fathers who stay at home to look after their children up to the age of five, is proposed by Michael Young and A H Halsey in their pamphlet *Family and Community Socialism* (London: Institute for Public Policy Research, 1995).

39. A Duncan *et al*, *The Impact of Subsidising Childcare*, Equal Opportunities Commission Research Discussion Series No 13 (Manchester: EOC, 1995).

40. H Seifert, 'Beschäftigungswirkungen und Perspektiven der Arbeitszeitpolitik', WSI *Mitteilungen*, No 3, 1989, cited in Hewitt, *About Time, op cit*, p91. For similar evidence from the UK, see R Richardson and M Rubin, 'The Economic Effects of Reductions in Working Hours: The UK Engineering Industry', *Research Series* No 34, Employment Department, 1994.

41. R. Freeman, 'The Limits of Wage Flexibility to Curing Unemployment', *Oxford Review of Economic Policy*, Vol 11, No 1, 1995, pp63–72.

42. D Card and A Krueger, *Myth and Measurement: The New Economics of the Minimum Wage* (Princeton, NJ: Princeton University Press, 1995). For a survey see G Burtless, 'Minimum Wages in the US', *New Economy*, Vol 2, No 4, 1995, pp204–209.

43. A Gosling, S Machin and C Meghir, *What's Happened to Wages?* (London: Institute for Fiscal Studies, 1994).

44. Department of Social Security, *Social Security Departmental Report: The Government's Expenditure Plans 1996/96–1997/98*, Cmnd 2813 (London: HMSO, 1995). This is the planned figure for 1995–96. It is planned to rise to £1.9 billion by 1997–98.

45. Central Statistical Office, NOMIS on-line database, December 1995.

46. R Layard, S Nickell and R Jackman, *Unemployment, Macroeconomic Performace and the Labour Market* (Oxford: Oxford University Press, 1991).

47 R Layard, *Preventing Long-Term Unemployment* (London: Employment Policy Institute, 1995).

Real World Member Organisations

Real World can be contacted c/o TCPA,
17 Carlton House Terrace,
London SW1Y 5AS
Tel: 0171 930 0375 Fax: 0171 930 3280

Readers wanting information about Real World's national and local activities can write to Real World (enclosing a medium-sized stamped addressed envelope). Alternatively, if you already have contact with one of the member organisations of the coalition, you may prefer to contact them instead; please make it clear when you write or phone that your enquiry is about Real World.

ALARM UK

9–10 College Terrace, London E3 5AN
Tel: 0181 983 3572   Fax: 0181 983 3572

ALARM UK is the umbrella body for around 250 local groups who have been opposing roadbuilding schemes. ALARM UK was founded in 1991, having started life as ALARM in London in the late 1980s. It campaigns for a sustainable transport policy.

Birmingham Settlement

318 Summer Lane, Birmingham B19 3RL
Tel: 0121 359 3562   Fax: 0121 359 6357

Birmingham Settlement has been working since 1899 to empower individuals and local communities, seeking to combat disadvantage and discrimination, fostering change and innovation.

Black Environment Network

9 Llainwen Uchaf, Llanberis, Wales LL55 4LL
Tel/Fax: 01286 870715

The Black Environment Network is established to enable black and white ethnic communities to participate fully in the preservation, protection and development of the environment. It maintains a UK-wide network of over 250 organisations and individuals working for change.

British Association of Settlements and Social Action Centres

1st Floor, Winchester House, 11 Cramner Road, London SW9 6EJ
Tel: 0171 735 1075   Fax: 0171 735 0840

BASSAC was founded in 1920 as the national body representing Settlements. It now has nearly 70 members and between them they support 1000 pieces of work. It is one of the key players in creating a community-based policy for urban renewal and regeneration.

Catholic Institute for International Relations

Unit 3, Canonbury Yard, 190a New North Road, Islington, London N1 7BJ
Tel: 0171 354 0883   Fax: 0171 359 0017
Email: internet:ciirlon@gn.apc.org or internet:ciir@geo2.poptel.org.uk

The Catholic Institute for International Relations, founded in 1940 by Cardinal Hinsley, is an independent charity working for justice and development. It specialises in skill-sharing, advocacy, information and analysis with, and on behalf of, its partners in the South. CIIR has 140 development workers overseas and 2,700 members.

Charter 88

Exmouth House, 3-11 Pine Street, London EC1R 0JH
Tel: 0171 833 1988   Fax: 0171 833 5895
Email: charter88@gn.apc.org

Charter 88 campaigns for constitutional reform and democratic renewal. Supported by over 60,000 signatories, it calls for a Bill of Rights, freedom of information, a fair voting system of proportional representation, Parliaments for Scotland and Wales, regional government, independence for local government, reform of the House of Commons, a democratic second chamber, reform of the judiciary, means of redress for state abuse – and a written constitution.

Christian Aid

PO Box 100, London SE1 7RT
Tel: 0171 620 4444   Fax: 0171 620 0719
Email: caid@gn.apc.org

Christian Aid is the official relief and development agency of 40 British and Irish Churches and works where the need is greatest in more than 70 countries worldwide. It helps communities of all religions and none. Christian Aid links directly with the poor through local organisations whose programmes aim to strengthen the poor towards self-sufficiency. It also seeks to address the root causes of poverty and spends up to 10 per cent of its income on development education and related campaigning at home. Over 300,000 people act as collectors for Christian Aid week.

Church Action on Poverty

Central Buildings, Oldham Street, Manchester M1 1JT
Tel: 0161 236 9321   Fax: 0161 237 5359

Church Action on Poverty was formed in 1982 as a Christian-based, ecumenical response to increasing levels of poverty in the UK. It is committed to a programme of theological reflection linked to educational and campaigning work. With around 2000 individual and group members CAP maintains active links with all the main Christian denominations and with many other church-based and secular social justice networks.

Employment Policy Institute

Southbank House, Black Prince Road, London SE1 7SJ
Tel: 0171 735 0777   Fax: 0171 735 1555
Email: 100130.2374@compuserve.com

The Employment Policy Institute (EPI) was founded in 1992 from the merging of the Employment Institute and Campaign for Work. As an independent think tank the EPI stands at the interface between academic research and practical policy making. The EPI aims to use the power of ideas to make a difference to the conduct of employment policy. It has 1000 subscribers.

Forum for the Future

Thornbury House, 18 High Street, Cheltenham GL50 1DZ
Tel: 01242 262737   Fax: 01242 262757

Forum for the Future is a new UK charity set up with the explicit purpose of taking a positive, solutions-orientated approach to today's environmental problems. It currently has five principal activities: a Scholarships scheme for young people; a Best Practice Database across a wide range of sustainability issues; a Sustainable Economy Unit, promoting economic solutions to environmental problems; a flagship publication called Green Futures; and a strategic consultancy service for businesses, local authorities and professional associations.

Friends of the Earth (England, Wales and Northern Ireland)

26-28 Underwood Street, London N1 7JQ
Tel: 0171 490 1555   Fax: 0171 490 0881

Friends of the Earth is one of the UK's leading environmental pressure groups, campaigning on a wide range of issues including pollution, transport, energy, waste, habitats, forests and sustainable development. Friends of the Earth exists to protect and improve the environment, now and for the future, through changing political policies and business practices, empowering individuals and communities to take personal and political action, and stimulating wide and intelligent public debate. Friends of the Earth has approximately 200,000 supporters and members, and over 250 local groups.

Friends of the Earth Scotland

Bonnington Mill, 72 Newhaven Road, Edinburgh EH6 5QG
Tel: 0131 554 9977   Fax: 0131 554 8656
Email: foescotland@gn.apc.org

FoE Scotland is an independent member of the Friends of the Earth International network. A research and campaigning organisation with 5000 members, its 'Towards a Sustainable Scotland' project is one of the first to mesh the environmental and social agendas. 10 staff and 20 volunteers are based in its offices in Edinburgh where the major work areas include energy, mineral extraction, climate change, transport, air pollution, and local sustainable development planning.

Greater Manchester Centre for Voluntary Organisation

St Thomas Centre, Ardwick Green North, Manchester M12 6FZ
Tel: 0161 273 7451 Fax: 0161 273 8296

Greater Manchester Centre for Voluntary Organisation's mission is to support and develop the voluntary sector. It aims to do this by enhancing the organisational effectiveness of voluntary and community groups primarily concerned with overcoming disadvantage or discrimination and, to this end, acts on strategic and structural matters in the county, region and nationally.

International Institute for Environment and Development

3 Endsleigh Street, London WC1H 0DD
Tel: 0171 388 2117   Fax: 0171 388 2826
Email: iiedinfo@gn.apc.org

IIED is an independent, non-profit organisation which seeks to promote sustainable patterns of development through research, policy studies, consensus-building and public information. Focusing on the connections between economic development, the environment and human needs, the Institute's principal aim is to improve the management of natural resources so that countries of the South can improve living standards without jeopardising their natural resource base. IIED is an associate member of Real World.

KAIROS (Centre for a Sustainable Society)

The Rectory, Glencarse, Perth PH2 7LX
Tel: 01738 860386   Fax: 01738 860386

KAIROS is supported by the Scottish Churches together. It was instrumental in founding the Scottish Environmental Forum, and is now promoting a programme of education and policy formation called 'Vision 21'. This is both a citizens' initiative in community education for sustainable development, and a programme to involve the community in 'Local Agenda 21' throughout Scotland.

Media Natura Trust

21 Tower Street, London WC2H 9NS
Tel: 0171 240 4936   Fax: 0171 240 2291
Email: medianatura@gn.apc.org

Established in 1988, Media Natura is a non profit agency offering communications strategy and media production skills, primarily to environment and development organisations. Media Natura also organises the British Environment and Media Awards, The Quarterly Forum, The Green Grant Scheme and the One World 96 Conference and Awards.

Medical Action for Global Security (MEDACT)

601 Holloway Road, London N19 4DJ
Tel: 0171 272 2020 Fax: 0171 281 5717
Email: medact@gn.apc.org

MEDACT is a voluntary association of doctors and other health professionals in the UK working for the abolition of nuclear weapons, the promotion of peace and global security, the protection of the environment, and preventive medicine on a global scale. It has a membership of over 2300 from all branches of clinical, public health and academic medicine, nursing and allied health professions. It is the UK affiliate of International Physicians for the Prevention of Nuclear War (IPPNW) which won the Nobel Peace Prize in 1985. IPPNW has affiliates in some 80 nations.

National Peace Council

88 Islington High Street, London N1 8EG
Tel: 0171 354 5200 Fax: 0171 354 0033
Email; npc@gn.apc.org World Wide Web: www.gn.apc.org/npc

National Peace Council's concerns are wide ranging and include conflict resolution, disarmament, human rights, justice, security, equality, development and humanitarian aid. These concerns are reflected in the diverse activities of our 250 member organisations throughout the UK, which range from small local peace groups to local authorities and trade unions. NPC helps its members to project their interests through the media, and consolidates their work by organising joint campaigns and activities. At times of crisis NPC provides a clearing house for action and information. Membership is open to sympathetic organisations and interested individuals.

Neighbourhood Initiatives Foundation

The Poplars, Lightmoor, Telford TF4 3QN
Tel: 01952 590777   Fax: 01952 591771

The Neighbourhood Initiatives Foundation is a national charity specialising in community participation, training and development. It works with local authorities, housing associations, voluntary agencies and community groups. The organisation's main purpose, using its distinctive approach to community involvement, is to empower people to shape the future of their neighbourhoods, often in the more disadvantaged areas of the country, and in the process improve the quality of life within their communities.

New Economics Foundation

1st Floor, Vine Court, 112–116 Whitechapel Road, London E1 1JE
Tel: 0171 377 5696   Fax: 0171 377 5720
Email: neweconomics@gn.apc.org

The New Economics Foundation grew out of The Other Economic Summit (TOES), founded in 1984 and now held every year in parallel to the seven richest nations' economic summits. Current projects include social auditing, formulating alternative economic indicators, investigating community enterprise, energy conservation, spreading economic alternatives for Eastern Europe, researching links between economics, trade and the environment, linking faith and ethics to economics, understanding social investment and sustainable development. The Foundation has 1500 supporters.

Oxfam

Oxfam House, 274 Banbury Road, Oxford OX2 7DZ
Tel: 01865 311311   Fax: 01865 312600

Founded in 1942, Oxfam UK/Ireland works with poor people worldwide regardless of race or religion in their struggle against hunger, disease, exploitation and poverty, through relief, development, research and public education. Oxfam's programme today aims to help poor people claim their basic rights to employment, shelter, food, health and education; to recognise women's special needs and capabilities; to help people win a say in decisions which affect their lives; and to support their efforts to live in ways that won't destroy the environment. Oxfam has both paid staff and around 30,000 volunteers.

Pesticides Trust

Eurolink Centre; 49 Effra Road, London SW2 1BZ
Tel: 0171 274 8895 Fax: 0171 274 9084
Email: pesttrust@gn.apc.org

The Pesticides Trust is a charity concerned with the health and environmental effects of pesticides. It works nationally and internationally with the Pesticides Action Network. It aims to reduce the hazards from exposure to pesticides; to improve sustainable livelihoods for farmers and growers; and to promote alternatives to pesticides.

Population Concern

178–202 Great Portland Street, London W1N 5TB
Tel: 0171 631 1546   Fax: 0171 436 2143

Population Concern works in partnership with grass-roots organisations in 19 less developed countries, helping women in particular to increase their opportunities and rights by providing reproductive health care, including family planning information and services.

The Poverty Alliance

162 Buchanan Street, Glasgow G1 2LL
Tel: 0141 353 0440   Fax: 0141 353 0686

The Poverty Alliance is a registered charity which seeks to combat poverty through the promotion of strategic and collaborative action. Poverty Alliance members include community groups, voluntary organisations, local authorities and individual community activists who support our aims. Alliance activities include awareness raising, network development, project development and support and skills training for community leaders who are active in local anti-poverty initiatives. The Poverty Alliance provides a platform for its members to challenge policies and practices which keep people in poverty and prioritises work which empowers people living in poverty to combat poverty on their own behalf.

Public Health Alliance

138 Digbeth, Birmingham B5 6DR
Tel: 0121 643 7628   Fax: 0121 643 4541

The Public Health Alliance was founded in 1987 and exists to promote and defend public health. It campaigns for health promoting public policy at all levels of government. It has summarised the environmental, social and economic influences on health in its Charter for Public Health. Recent and current projects include work on sustainable development and health, poverty and health, primary care and the impact of crime on public health. There are 170 organisations in membership and 300 individuals.

Quaker Social Responsibility and Education

Friends House, 173–177 Euston Road, London NW1 2BJ
Tel: 0171 387 3601   Fax: 0171 388 1977

Quaker Social Responsibility and Education (QSRE) supports Quakers in Britain on issues of social/economic justice – including housing and penal reform – equality, democratic renewal, truth and integrity in public affairs and community care, and presents Quaker views nationally. QSRE works in tandem with Quaker Peace and Service (QPS) whose concerns include international conciliation and reconciliation, global economic values, the arms trade, and environmental sustainability. There are 18,000 Quaker members and 10,000 Attenders.

Save the Children Fund

17 Grove Lane, London SE5 8RD
Tel: 0171 703 5400   Fax: 0171 703 2278

The Save the Children Fund (SCF) is the UK's largest international voluntary agency concerned with child health and welfare. Founded in 1919, it works both in Britain and overseas to achieve lasting benefits for children within the communities in which they live. As well as its funded projects, SCF aims to influence policy and practice based on its experience and study in different parts of the world. In all of its work, Save the Children endeavours to make a reality of children's rights, working together with over 20,000 active supporters and the 24 sister organisations of the International Save the Children Alliance, with which it is affiliated worldwide.

Scottish Education and Action for Development (Sead)

23 Castle Street, Edinburgh EH2 3DN
Tel: 0131 225 6550   Fax: 0131 226 6384

Sead (Scottish Education and Action for Development) was established in 1978 to examine and compare the common roots of poverty and the linkages between the processes and experiences of development as they exist both in Scotland and in the world's poorer nations. It is a membership charity. It produces publications, organises conferences and study tours, runs campaigns, undertakes research and consultancy work and coordinates an international network to exchange ideas for action on development.

Sustainable Agriculture, Food and Environment (SAFE) Alliance

38 Ebury Street, London SW1W 0LU
Tel: 0171 823 5660   Fax: 0171 823 5673
Email: safe@gn.apc.org

The SAFE Alliance exists to unite farmer, environmental, consumer, animal welfare and development organisations. Its 33 member organisations share a common vision of food production which is beneficial to the environment, is sensitive to the need for global equity, and which produces safe, healthy and affordable food in a manner supportive of rural life and culture. Through analysis, research, education and information, the SAFE Alliance promotes sustainable food production and generates pressure for change. SAFE is part of a Network of Alliances across Europe.

Sustrans

35 King Street, Bristol BS1 4DZ

Tel: 0117 926 8893   Fax: 0117 929 4173

Sustrans is a practical charity which designs and builds routes for cyclists, walkers and people with disabilities. It has completed several hundred miles of traffic-free paths through urban and country areas and promotes Safe Routes to Schools. In partnership with local authorities and other bodies, Sustrans is now creating the 6500-mile National Cycle Network which was chosen by the Millennium Commission as a major project to mark the new millennium in September 1995. Sustrans has over 15,000 individual supporters, and hundreds of supporting bodies and partner organisations. Sustrans is working to bring about a society less dependent on the car.

Tools for Self Reliance

Netley Marsh, Southampton SO40 7GY

Tel: 01703 869 697 Fax: 01703 868 544

Email: tools@gn.apc.org

Tools for Self Reliance works with partner organisations in Sierra Leone, Ghana, Uganda, Tanzania, Zimbabwe, Mozambique, and Nicaragua. A network of UK volunteers refurbish unwanted hand tools and sewing machines which are then sent to artisan groups selected by the partner organisations. TFSR also works with certain partners to promote tool making in this country. It is also concerned with the causes of poverty and has a small development education programme operating in the UK. It has seven paid staff and volunteers actively collecting and refurbishing in over 150 places in Britain.

Town and Country Planning Association

17 Carlton House Terrace, London SW1Y 5AS

Tel: 0171 930 8903   Fax: 0171 930 3280

The Town and Country Planning Association is an independent charity which campaigns for improvements to the environment through effective planning, public participation and sustainable development. Founded in 1899 to spread the message of garden cities, it is Britain's oldest independent charity concerned with *people* and the built environment. Its membership is drawn equally from the corporate sector, local government and concerned individuals.

Transport 2000

Walkden House, 10 Melton Street, London NW1 3EJ

Tel: 0171 388 8386   Fax: 0171 388 2481

Transport 2000 is the national environmental transport campaign. It campaigns for a coherent and sustainable national transport policy which meets transport needs with least damage to the environment. Transport 2000 works to improve transport policy by research, reports, seminars and lobbying. It works at a national level and through its 35 local groups. Its membership is made up of affiliated organisations along with 1300 individuals and 30 corporate supporters.

Unemployment Unit

322 St John Street, London EC1V 4NT

Tel: 0171 833 1222   Fax: 0171 833 1121

Email: unemploy.unit@mcrl.poptel.org.uk

The Unemployment Unit is an independent organisation researching and campaigning on the problems facing the unemployed, in particular the long term and recurrently out of work. The Unit promotes economic policies likely to restore full employment and to counter discrimination in the labour market, better ameliorative measures, and for effective training and employment opportunities for the unemployed. The Unit organises seminars, conferences and training events, publishes a range of information and provides a wide range of free advice and information to unemployed people and trainees, to researchers, officers and Members in local government and to MPs of all parties.

United Nations Association

3 Whitehall Court, London SW1A 2EL

Tel: 0171 930 2931   Fax: 0171 930 5893

The United Nations Association was founded in 1945 to support and promote the work of the United Nations. The membership of UNA is about 7500, it has over 120 branches around the UK and is a member of the World Federation of UNAs with sister organisations in over 70 countries. The UNA Sustainable Development Unit has taken a lead in supporting community-based action on sustainability and works with both voluntary groups and local authorities on the local implementation of sustainable development. The SDU also acts as the Secretariat for UNED-UK, which monitors the implementation of Agenda 21. The UNA's other departments focus on Human Rights and on Refugees and Conflict Prevention.

Walter Segal Self Build Trust
Unit 213, 16 Baldwin Gardens, London EC1N 7RJ
Tel: 0171 831 5696 Fax: 0171 831 5697

The Walter Segal Self Build Trust is a national charity which helps people to build their own homes. The Trust's services are available to everyone, especially those in housing need or on low incomes, as individuals or in groups. The Trust has a strong belief in the power of self-build as a way of contributing to the improvement of local communities in many ways, not only by providing good quality, affordable housing, but also by providing training and skills to build strong communities in which to live.

The Wildlife Trusts
UK National Office, The Green, Witham Park, Waterside South, Lincoln LN5 7JR
Tel: 01522 544 400 Fax: 01522 511 616
Email: wildlifersnc@cix.compulink.co.uk World Wide Web:
http://www.wildlifetrust.org.uk

The Wildlife Trusts are a nationwide network of local trusts which work to protect wildlife in town and country. Through their care of 2000 nature reserves, The Wildlife Trusts are dedicated to the achievement of a UK richer in wildlife, managed on sustainable principles. Sharing this goal and making a vital contribution to its attainment are the junior branch, Wildlife Watch, and the urban wildlife groups around the country. Using their specialist skills in the fields of conservation and education, The Wildlife Trusts strive to win public recognition that the achievement of their aims is essential for a healthy environment and continued human existence.

Women's Environmental Network
87 Worship Street, London EC2A 2BE
Tel: 0171 247 3327 Fax: 0171 247 4740
Email: wenek@gn.apc.org

Women's Environmental Network seeks to educate, inform and empower women, and men, who care about the environment to take positive environmental action towards a more sustainable lifestyle. WEN provides well-researched, unbiased information about a range of consumer issues and is currently campaigning from a woman's perspective on air pollution, waste prevention, sanitary protection and biotechnology.

World Development Movement (WDM)
25 Beehive Place, London SW9 7QR
Tel: 0171 737 6215   Fax: 0171 274 8232

WDM aims to achieve justice for the world's poorest people through campaigns that tackle the fundamental causes of poverty. WDM is a democratic nationwide network of members and groups campaigning with groups in World. We are not a charity and can campaign in ways that charities can't. We campaign for: controls on the arms trade, better quality and quantity of aid; cancellation of Third World debt; fair trade and controls on multi-nationals. Ou goal is to create the conditions that will enable the world's poorest people to achieve equitable and sustainable development.

World Wide Fund for Nature (WWF) UK
Panda House, Weyside Park, Godalming GU7 1XR
Tel: 01483 426444   Fax: 01483 426409

The World Wide Fund for Nature (WWF) works in over 100 countries to conserve biodiversity, promote sustainable development and reduce pollution and wasteful consumption. In addition to programmes for policy reform, education and capacity-building, WWF undertakes or supports thousands of practical projects. Most of these are working with local communities to help them improve standards of living through sustainable management of their resources. WWF's ultimate goal is to build a future in which people live in harmony with nature. In the UK, WWF has 220,000 members. The international membership of WWF numbers over 2 million.

NB. In addition to their members, subscribers and volunteers, the member organisations of Real World have between them over 1.25 million identified financial supporters.